Organizational Hybridity and Social Innovation

Three Essays on the Management of Social and Economic Impact in Social Enterprises and Social Impact Incubators and Accelerators

Lucca Nietlispach

Bibliografische Information der Deutschen Nationalbibliothek: Die Deutsche Nationalbibliothek verzeichnet diese Publikation in der Deutschen Nationalbibliografie; detaillierte bibliografische Daten sind im Internet über dnb.dnb.de abrufbar.

Verlag: BoD · Books on Demand GmbH, In de Tarpen 42, 22848 Norderstedt

Druck: Libri Plureos GmbH, Friedensallee 273, 22763 Hamburg

ISBN: 978-3-7597-4992-5

Table of Contents

Acknowledgements

Undertaking a journey to write a dissertation undoubtedly and unsurprisingly has many challenges. As my grandfather likes to point out: "Von nix kommt nix!". At this stage, I am already starting to see a return on my investment. I am sure that I will profit my entire life from the knowledge and experience I obtained. This whole journey is closely connected to the people that accompanied me during this time, and I extend my heartfelt gratitude to them.

First, I would like to thank Prof. Dr. Georg von Schnurbein for taking great care to always be available for support when challenges arose. His advice, feedback and guidance contributed in numerous ways to my thesis, as well as to my personal development. My gratitude also goes out to Prof. Dr. Michael Meyer for taking on the role of my second supervisor. His encouragement in discussions at conferences, as well as the connection to various researchers at WU Vienna was valuable. Furthermore, I want to express my gratitude to all the researchers around the world that I met at conferences and contributed with their feedback to this thesis. In addition, the second essay would not have been possible without the kind collaboration of the Social Innovation Lab in Freiburg, Germany. Special thanks go out to Corinna Kämpfe and Jella Riesterer for their support in conducting my case study. I would also like to thank all the anonymous professionals from the social impact community for answering the survey without which this research could have not been completed.

Furthermore, I am extremely grateful to the whole CEPS team. Many formal and informal discussions were helpful to get the mind out of its occasional ruts and back to creative problem solving. Many current and former employees have become dear friends and I am sure that we will stay in touch the next years and decades. I thank one former colleague in particular: Carina Greussing has become my partner and I am endlessly grateful for the love and support that she has given me and continues to give me every day.

I could not have written this thesis without my family and friends. My parents and grandparents were always there for me when I needed to take a break from research and clear the mind from old ideas, such that new and better ones were able to enter. I thank my mother, Nicole Nietlispach, for her unconditional support, my grandmother, Helga Ertl, for sparking my curiosity in reading, my father, Pius Nietlispach, for teaching me what is important and my grandfather, Rainer Ertl, for pushing me and always believing in me. I also thank one of the kindest people that I knew, my grandmother, Marie Nietlispach. Moreover, I am filled with gratitude for the best siblings an older brother could ask for, thank you Noah and Saskia! Last but not least, I would like to thank my friends for taking an interest in my academic projects and contributing their knowledge of the various fields that they specialized in over the last decade.

Preface

Introduction

Society currently faces many challenges that will have to be addressed in the next decades. Growing population numbers challenge the food system (Fresco, 2009), health care costs are steadily increasing (BFS, 2023) and fossil fuels have to be replaced by renewable energy (Abas et al., 2015). There are no easy and straight-forward solutions to these challenges. Most importantly, viable solutions need to encompass both social and economic aspects. For example, they must consider the needs of many stakeholders, but also regard efficiency and cost reduction as important. Modern theories ascribe social and economic value creation to different sectors. On the one hand, social value is prototypically pursued by the third sector, made up mostly of nonprofit organizations. On the other hand, economic value is created by the private sector, which is made up of profit-oriented companies. However, an increasing number of organizations aim to create both social and economic value in conjunction. These organizations are hybrid in nature and are not easily categorized in one sector. This difficulty in categorization creates legitimacy challenges. In addition, hybrid organizations have to overcome obstacles particularly when targeting growth and the dissemination of a particular innovative approach or product. Struggles arise because social and economic orientations are often in contest with each other. Economic success is often lowered when social responsibility is maximized and mission drift is a concern for economically focused organizations (Hersberger-Langloh et al., 2021). However, hybrid organizations are seen as potentially effective approaches to sustainable development. These organizations internalize the complexity of challenges. Hence, the pressure to innovate is created instead of the prescription to established business or nonprofit practices. Organizational hybridity and its role in social innovation is also an area of interest in politics. For example, the "Social Economy Action Plan" published by the European Commission (2021) aims to support the social economy in order to promote innovation and the creation of jobs. More resources are directed towards the joint pursuit of social and economic value. However, policy-making is at its very early stages in regards to recognizing hybrid organizations at the intersection of social and economic value creation (Humbel & Wittkämpfer, 2024). Thus, the ecosystem that is forming through and around these organizations is connected and supported largely by private organizations. Initiatives like B Lab certify social enterprises as "B-Corp" firms which signals their adherence to standards of social and economic aspects (Chen & Kelly, 2015). This can alleviate some of the legitimacy concerns. In addition, private intermediary organizations such as social impact incubators and accelerators (SIIAs) also step in to support hybrid organizations in their growth aspirations.

Apart from the requirements by private certifications, there are only few managerial guidelines for hybrid organizations like social enterprises. What would a holistic approach to hybrid governance look like? Beyond the organizational level, further challenges arise. How do interactions take place in hybrid environments? How can divergent perspectives be overcome? How can interactions be shaped in order to facilitate mutual learning? In addition, the question arises how these endeavors can and should be funded. Hybrid organizations can be less attractive for investors because of their limited profit orientation, but they are also not eligible for tax exemption. Which organizations remain to be targeted as potential funders?

These questions are at the center of this thesis. In order to contextualize the three essays comprising the thesis, I first elaborate on the relevance of the topic overall. I also introduce the individual research questions which guided the three essays. Then, I build a conceptual basis for how the individual studies are related to each other and illustrate this graphically. In addition, I explain the approach and overall process taken in the development of the thesis. I also discuss the results and final output of the research before critically assessing its contribution, practical implications and limitations.

Relevance and Research Questions

The pursuit of multiple objectives has become a topic of investigation in many research fields. It is a major focus of research in the social innovation (Bethmann, 2020; Mulgan, 2006), social entrepreneurship (Saebi et al., 2019) and social enterprise (Ebrahim et al., 2014) fields. On the one hand, scholars researching social entrepreneurship focus on the skills and activities of individual entrepreneurs and their abilities to create social and economic value (Jin, 2020; Siegner et al., 2018). On the other hand, social innovation research is focused more on processes of innovation (Mulgan, 2006). Transformative social innovation goes beyond the individual and organizational level (Audretsch et al., 2021). Collaborations between a multitude of actors are investigated (Voltan & De Fuentes, 2016). Further, social enterprise research has developed in order to study these dual pursuits in organizational form. In Europe, many social enterprises are young organizations with more than 80% of organizations founded in the last 20 years. Health and social work, as well as education, are major fields of activity of European social enterprises (Dupain et al., 2022).

Social enterprises are regarded as the most prominent example of a hybrid organization (Alberti & Varon Garrido, 2017; Haigh & Hoffman, 2014). However, the social enterprise label is very broad. The orientations of social enterprises and their goals vary significantly. A social purpose organization that takes the opportunity to generate a small share of earned income is a hybrid organization because the participation in market activities necessitates economic in addition to social considerations. For example, this organization needs to pay heed to seasonal changes in demand and possibly take up marketing activities. However, this organization's identity hinges on the social purpose and not the sales of a minor product or service that it took up opportunistically. The nature of hybridity is different for an organization that is financially self-sustaining but also has clear and non-negotiable metrics for social objectives. This variety in the nature of social enterprises is the reason that recent research has called for a differentiation of degrees of hybridity in organizations (Battilana et al., 2017). With a greater understanding of different degrees of hybridity, there is also an increased need to differentiate the management in hybrid organizations. In the literature, various strategies for successful management of hybridity are identified (Battilana et al., 2017). However, these are often not based in an understanding of different degrees of hybridity. A comprehensive approach necessitates a portfolio of strategies that need to be considered and possibly applied in conjunction. A systematic approach is warranted which facilitates a synergetic relationship between social and economic aspects. In essay one, I ask how the current literature can inform such a framework to manage hybridity based on degree.

Similar to most other organizations participating in market activities, hybrid organizations aim to grow. Social enterprises in particular are rather young organizations with strong growth aspirations (Dupain et al., 2022). In order to increase their chances of this undertaking, they often participate in support programs (Lall et al., 2020). These so-called incubation and acceleration programs have gained increasing relevance (Kerlin et al., 2021). Programs usually span several months and are often conducted yearly with cohorts of organizations. Participants usually get chosen based on a set of selection criteria (Hirschmann et al., 2021). On average, about a dozen participants take part in one program (Lall et al., 2020). Besides regular workshops and personal mentoring, the program offers participants a connection to the network of the incubator and accelerator environment. The environment of these programs is characterized by institutional complexity. Not only do managers and program participants have potentially conflicting orientations, but many other organizations are part of this environment. Even though previous literature indicates the importance of learning for the development of hybrid organizations (Knutsson & Thomasson, 2017) and the value social entrepreneurs see in accelerators (Pandey et al., 2017), there is limited knowledge of the dynamics. These programs provide a fertile research context to understand how individuals behave in environments of institutional complexity when numerous hybrid organizations interact. Particularly, interactions of program managers with program participants are a black box. Thus, I ask how interaction and the learning process take place in SIIAs. In the results of the study, I describe how programs can be improved and what should be considered when selecting participants. Both understanding incubation and acceleration programs with a social goal, as well as contexts of institutional complexity is highly relevant beyond the setting of hybrid organizations. Other actors such as nonprofit organizations and companies are increasingly involved in these types of networks.

Lastly, the third essay also sheds light on the institutional complexity of the operation of SIIA programs. However, the focus is explicitly on managerial challenges in terms of funding incubation and acceleration programs in hybrid contexts. This is highly relevant, as all hybrid organizations face challenges to target and receive adequate funding. The boundaries of their social and economic value creation are not clear. The benefits they provide are varied and can possibly attract various funders. This leads to funding relationships in the context of SIIAs that are not based on any well-known prototype. For example, corporate foundations might provide donations to business programs in their specific fields in order to promote innovation in that industry. However, corporate foundations also provide donations to nonprofit organizations as part of their philanthropic initiatives. In addition, business startups are possibly supported by nonprofit organizations and not only companies. The rise of hybrid legal forms in many countries has created additional complexity. Hence, there is little knowledge on the relationship between the benefits that an organization provides and its relationship to funding. Thus, essay three asks how the benefits provided by SIIAs influence their funding mix.

All three articles are concerned with the challenge of navigating an environment of institutional complexity in which social and economic pursuits take center stage. This thesis' direction of movement is from an organizational focus on social enterprises to studying interactions between social enterprises and SIIAs in an incubator program to an organizational focus on SIIAs (Table 1). It develops from an exploratory and conceptual to an explanatory and empirical approach. As managing social responsibility becomes more important for businesses and nonprofit organizations face increased pressures of marketization, the implications of this thesis go beyond the application to hybrid organizations only.

Main Research Questions		Organizational Focus	Aim / Type
Essay 1	How can hybridity be managed systematically?	Social enterprises	Exploratory / Conceptual
Essay 2	How do interactions and the learning process take place in social impact incubator programs?	Social impact incubator program	Exploratory / Qualitative empirical
Essay 3	How do the benefits provided by social impact incubators and accelerators affect the composition of their revenue sources?	Social impact incubators and accelerators	Explanatory / Quantitative empirical

Table 1: Thesis overview with main research questions and type of essays

Conceptual Structure and Central Theories

A number of theories and concepts underlie the individual essays. In order to contextualize the research setting and the dynamics that take place within it, this section elaborates on the central theories and concepts and illustrates their interconnectedness (Figure 1). In addition, the roles of SIIAs are further elaborated because of the importance they have in this thesis.

Social impact incubators and accelerators (SIIAs) are intermediaries in innovation ecosystems (Domanski et al., 2019; Howells, 2006). They are most known for the cyclical programs they provide to cohorts of organizations. In these programs, SIIA managers personally mentor and train participants to help them develop their organizations. SIIAs are also network hubs where diverse actors come together: founders, investors, and consultants find opportunities to pursue their interests. Additionally, the general public is invited to events and pitches. Moreover, local political actors are often interested in the development of these organizations. Overall, SIIAs are characterized by a convening of diverse stakeholders that ranges from social activists to venture capitalists. The central goal of SIIAs is ultimately directed towards disseminating social innovation. Simply put, SIIAs conduct their programs and adjacent services to promote social enterprises in their pursuit of addressing a social issue.

Many presentations, events, informal talks, and projects revolve around the intersection of social and economic orientations. Undoubtedly, the institutional environment of SIIAs is hybrid. The simplest way to conceptualize hybridity regards social and economic aspects as the ends of a continuous spectrum. SIIAs at one end of this spectrum have a strong focus on social aspects, while those at the other end focus on economic aspects to a large degree. Hybrid organizations are typically positioned around the middle of this spectrum, with a more or less equal prioritization of these two aspects. SIIAs can vary in their placement on the spectrum depending on the strength of each aspect within the organization.

The position of SIIAs on this spectrum influences the suitability of different funding sources. Social impact is increasingly important for investors, and nonprofit organizations are seeking alternative and more entrepreneurial grant-making models. Thus, SIIAs can potentially be funded by a wide range of organizations. However, without being able to clearly target funding organizations based on their degree of hybridity, SIIAs have difficulties in receiving funding. Benefits theory of nonprofit finance helps SIIAs understand the benefits of their services and, consequently, enables them to communicate their value creation to targeted funding organizations (Young, 2017). Benefits theory suggests a relationship between the benefits of organizations and their funding sources. In the context of SIIAs, an organization that offers private benefits and private goods should be predominantly funded by earned income, while SIIAs offering social benefits for specific groups should be funded by donation income. The assessment of the type of benefit is best made by understanding the nature of participants in incubation and acceleration programs.

As laid out, the operation of programs is an important part of managing an SIIA. However, this extends beyond funding. To conduct a program successfully, one must understand the dynamics between incubator managers and program participants in greater detail. Structuration theory provides a suitable theoretical foundation for understanding the dynamic nature of these interactions (Giddens, 1986). Structuration theory has been applied to social innovation research before (Cajaiba-Santana, 2010). It is suitable because it takes into consideration the interdependence between structure and agency over longer time spans. This is apt for understanding social innovation processes that are complex and long-lasting. (Murray et al., 2010).

In structuration theory, structure is understood to encompass both material resources and mental knowledge structures (Sewell, 1992). Program participants are affected by existing structures in the sense that programs have a predetermined itinerary. Participants receive various resources during the program, including office space, templates, and sometimes even financial resources. While mental knowledge structures are less prominent, they are equally important. Participants are exposed to new ways of thinking and problem-solving, akin to the provision of material resources. Similar to material resources, participants choose which knowledge structures are helpful, which to discard, or even which to regard negatively.

Agency comprises both habitual and purposive actions of individuals (Sarason et al., 2006). Applied to the case of SIIAs, the focus lies on the agency of program participants and their potential to influence existing structures they regard as problematic. Program participants, as agents, purposefully aim to change these existing structures.

Structuration theory is helpful in understanding these foundational yet general principles that guide interactions. In order to delve into specific characteristics influencing this dynamic, different dimensions of program participants' proximity to the SIIA program are considered in addition to structuration theory. Proximity research has roots in the field of economic geography (Boschma, 2005), and various areas of innovation research have applied the concept to understand interactions between agents in innovation processes (Balland et al., 2015). Not only spatial proximity but also cognitive, social, and institutional forms of proximity are important. For example, some participants are rarely present in the physical facilities during the program but exhibit great cognitive proximity, being very familiar with the methods of social entrepreneurship. In this way, one form of proximity might be substituted for another.

Insights into the varied dynamics of SIIA programs illustrate the multifaceted approaches of organizations. The multitude of diverse outcomes for organizations should caution against assuming simple relationships between social and economic aspects. The continuum approach is a zero-sum game and implies that an increase in one aspect leads to a decrease in the other. Some scholars have questioned this approach to hybridity (Teasdale, 2012) because several organizations are successful examples of both social and economic value creation. For example, Fairphone is a social enterprise that produces a smartphone that is socially "fair" (Cornelissen et al., 2021). Most importantly, it addresses concerns regarding conflict minerals in smartphones (Akemu et al., 2016). Another successful example of a social enterprise is Digital Divide Data (Smith & Besharov, 2019). It supports socially disadvantaged employees in the Southeast Asian context in various ways. Organizations like these are committed to a high level of both social and economic value creation. They operate at scale and impose clear metrics and guidelines for achieving a social mission. Thus, the conceptualization of hybridity as a continuum captures only a small portion of the phenomenon.

In response to these developments, Shepherd et al. (2019) developed a framework that allows for the assessment of more varied degrees of hybridity. They assess hybridity along two dimensions rather than only one. The most significant change to the continuum approach is that a high level of intensity in one aspect does not necessarily imply a low level in the other. As explained, research on successful social enterprises has shown how some organizations achieve a balance of higher intensity than others. Thus, the intensity of either aspect is assessed separately. This leads organizations to display different degrees of hybridity. In addition to the intensity of either logic, their relative relationship can be analyzed as well. High relative hybridity is exhibited by organizations that equally prioritize social and economic aspects.

Although frameworks by Shepherd et al. (2019) and others (Besharov & Smith, 2014) provide insights into hybrid organizations, they remain rather conceptual and not connected to strategy and management. In addition, the literature in the field of hybridity management in social enterprises has grown, but it is fragmented. Various strategies of integration (Cornforth, 2014) and differentiation (Siegner et al., 2018) are discussed. For example, organizations are not always stable in terms of their social or economic orientation. They can oscillate, particularly over long time spans (Kurland & Schneper, 2021). In order to provide a conceptual basis for these different strategies, the recent literature on the management of hybridity in social enterprises is investigated in detail based on Shepherd et al.'s (2019) framework.

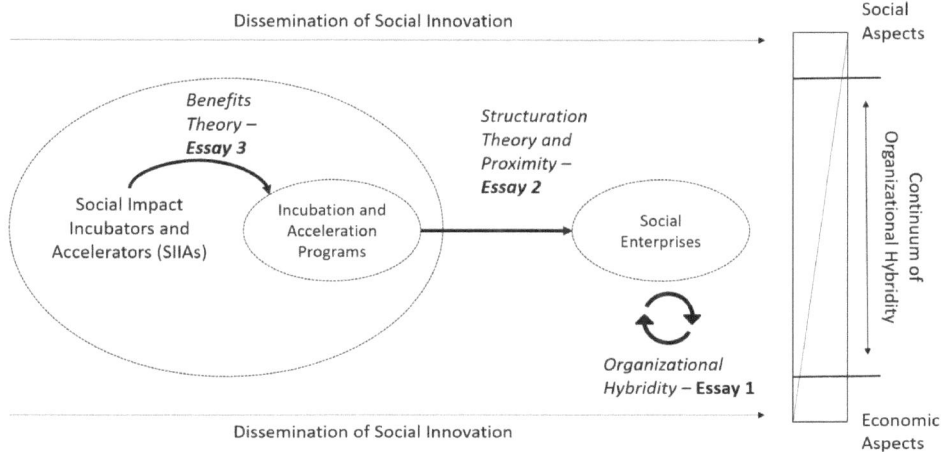

Figure 1: Theories and central concepts underlying the thesis (own illustration)

Research Approach and Process

The initial starting point for the development of this thesis was the submission of a research proposal nine months into the process. In the research proposal, the relationship between social and economic aspects in social innovation processes and the discussion of a blurring of sectors laid the groundwork for the subsequent focus of the thesis. The research proposal also included a preliminary outline for the three essays. By the time of submission of the research proposal, the sampling of articles for the literature review in essay one had been concluded. I had already included some descriptive statistics and a tentative discussion of hybridity management strategies. Further, the research concept for essay two had been planned. The focus on SIIAs as a particularly fruitful context for understanding disseminations of social innovation had been decided. Thus, the research proposal also contained a literature review of SIIAs.

Essay one "*A Framework for Managing Hybridity in Social Enterprises*" is conceptual in nature. It assesses the literature of hybridity management through the method of a systematic literature review. The advantages of conducting a literature review systematically are the clear guidelines for the process and the traceability of findings and conclusions. Web of Science and Scopus served as sources for scientific articles investigating this issue. After defining the search keywords and inclusion and exclusion criteria, 82 relevant articles were identified. Only peer-reviewed articles published in or after the year 2012 were included. The goal of the review was to assess the current state of the literature on hybridity management in social enterprises. Working with the citation program EndNote, as well as the coding program MAXQDA allowed me to quantitatively assess and describe this sample of articles. First, a sample of 25 articles was coded with a preliminary set of codes. After assessing the findings of the first round of coding, additional codes were added. Several rounds of coding of all articles was conducted in the next step. The process of manual coding led to a list of central strategies of hybridity management from each paper. Descriptive statistics were laid out through a content analysis (Bengtsson, 2016; Krippendorff, 2004). Qualitative meta-analysis allowed to organize the findings across the different studies and relate them to Shepherd et al.'s (2019) conceptual framework (Timulak, 2009, 2014).

Scaling and the ambition to grow was identified to be a central goal of social enterprises in the literature review (Gibbons & Hazy, 2017; Kannothra et al., 2018; Sarhangi et al., 2021; Siebold et al., 2019; Yin & Chen, 2019). Hence, in essay two *"From Social Worker to Social Entrepreneur: Dynamic Proximity in a Social Impact Incubator"*, more emphasis was placed on processes of dissemination of social innovation. Social impact incubators and accelerators were determined early on to be a fruitful setting for studying the aspirations of social entrepreneurs to address a social problem. In particular, interactions and the learning process of participants in these programs was identified as a research gap. Subsequently, a suitable research setting needed to be determined for conducting the investigation. A few organizations were contacted in the process. Among those was also the Social Innovation Lab in Freiburg, Germany. The request to collaborate for a case study was sent via email to the organization in January, 2022. The initial contact led me to be referred to the program manager of the "Sozialstarter"-program. I presented the goals of my research and we were able to reach an agreement on the terms and conditions of the research engagement. This written agreement was signed a few days after initial contact. The program itself took place from March to July 2022. The research process took place in two central stages. In the first phase, data collection focused on participant observation in the programs. I was allowed to participate in all of the program workshops, which took place at the rate of about once per month. I was able to collect data through gathering field notes in participant observation. The managers and staff in the program were collaborative and shared all types of documentation on the program. I received recordings of pre-meetings with participants, all the presentations of the workshops and program application details. I was also included in the email communication to participants. In addition, I conducted preliminary interviews with program participants and incubator managers. The majority of the interviews was conducted in the second phase of data collection. The second phase took place in the six months following the final pitches and end of the program. I conducted a total of 15 interviews during and after the program with incubator staff. The second phase of interviews was conducted with program participants only. The interviews were conducted mostly in separate visits to the Social Innovation Lab. These separate visits further allowed to gather insights into the environment of the incubator program through participant observation. In the end, this longitudinal approach led to the collection of data over the span of 10 months. The gathered data is analyzed with the Gioia method (Gioia, 2021; Gioia et al., 2013). Based on the theoretical framework of structuration theory and proximity research, I conducted several rounds of descriptive and open coding. After identifying first-order codes, these were aggregated to second-order themes, and ultimately, to the two aggregate dimensions of proximity augmentation and proximity moderation.

Finally, essay three *"Revenue Streams of Social Impact Incubators and Accelerators: The Influence of Program Benefits"* takes a closer look at how SIIA programs are financed. This study is co-authored by my supervisor Georg von Schnurbein. We investigate how the benefits of SIIA programs influence their funding based on benefits theory. Benefits theory of nonprofit finance anticipates how organizations secure funding, suggesting a relationship between funding origins and the benefits offered. For instance, a nonprofit focusing on public services is inclined to receive funding from governmental sources (Young, 2017). In this study, we investigate the effect of providing social versus economic benefits and what effect this has on earned income, government income and donation income.

Social and economic aspects are salient in multiple organizational aspects. In this essay, we focus particularly on organizational identity and attention to goals in order to assess organizational hybridity. On the one hand, organizational identity is a frequently applied theoretical perspective to study hybrid organizations (Smith et al., 2013). Organizational identity is "the set of beliefs about what is most core, enduring, and distinctive about an organization" (Voss et al., 2006, p. 741). On the other hand, attention needs to be divided constantly among goals in organizations which is the reason for the interest of researchers in this topic (Ocasio, 1997; Stevens et al., 2015). In particular, attention to social goals has become more important for organizations in particular (Kurland & Schneper, 2021; Sarma, 2020). We hypothesize a negative effect of a focus of SIIAs on program participants' economic organizational identity on the attention to social goals of program participants because of the literature indicating tensions between social and economic missions (Dufays, 2019; Joseph et al., 2020).

Data was collected through a global survey. The questionnaire was developed on Qualtrics. Survey drafts were discussed and tested with two practitioners in the SIIA field. The identification of relevant survey respondents was based on webscraping. Email addresses were identified through three different sources. First, LinkedIn was scraped to identify SIIAs. Second, a list of website addresses of social enterprise incubators from a landscape report (Sours et al., 2020) was used. Third, the Global Accelerator Learning Initiative (GALI) directory was scraped. Most potential respondents were identified through LinkedIn. The survey was sent to a total of 2232 email addresses, of which 127 filled in the survey in a span of about seven weeks from August to October 2023. The low response rate speaks to the difficulty of collecting survey data in this context. The data was analyzed in RStudio and modeled in a partial least squares structural equation model. The model was estimated with a sample of 89 organizations due to the necessary exclusion of many responses. List-wise deletion was necessary because of missing financial data in most cases. The model includes the effects of economic organizational identity and attention to social goals on the most central funding sources for SIIAs: earned income, government income and donation income. By investigating these effects and identifying significant relationships, we can form recommendations for funding in SIIAs. The next section will go into the specifics of the findings of this essay, as well as the previous two.

Research Output

The aim of the first essay of this thesis ("*A Framework for Managing Hybridity in Social Enterprises*") was to investigate the strategies of hybridity management in social enterprises through a systematic literature review. The output of this essay are descriptive statistics on this literature, general research orientations of the field and a framework to manage hybridity comprehensively. The descriptive statistics indicate that there has been a rise in publications that study hybridity management in social enterprises in recent years. Prominent publishing journals in the field are the Journal of Business Ethics, the Social Enterprise Journal and the Journal of Social Entrepreneurship. Most studies apply a multiple case study approach. Further, three specific scholarly research orientations were identified in which articles were grouped. The first group of articles is focused on social entrepreneurs and their skills. The second group is focused on a particular management area, such as governance and boards or supply chain management. The third group of articles is holistically focused on identifying a set of guiding principles that guide hybridity management in social enterprises. The main result of the essay is the conceptualization of a framework to manage hybridity in social enterprises. The framework builds on the framework by Shepherd et al. (2019) and identifies three central aspects: (1) positioning regarding relative hybridity, (2) the setting of guardrails to avoid excessively low relative hybridity and (3) the efforts to increase the degree of hybridity. First, social enterprises need to be aware of different levels of relative hybridity they can exhibit. While some SEs aim to prioritize social and economic aspects equally, others explicitly regard either social or economic aspects to be more important. However, when one aspect is prioritized, guardrails need to be put in place to ensure relative hybridity stays within certain boundaries. Hence, setting guardrails is the second category of the framework. These guardrails can for instance be negotiation spaces (Battilana et al., 2015), rituals of conflict management (Ashforth & Reingen, 2014) or strategic and legal guidelines such as byelaws (Bruneel et al., 2020; Sanzo-Pérez et al., 2021). Third, hybrid organizations that strive for growth and an increase of the degree of hybridity need to be aware of the importance of a clear vision. A long-term perspective is necessary to reap advantages of a hybrid approach.

The first essay was presented at the seminar in social entrepreneurship and philanthropy (SE-PHI) in May, 2023 in Paris, France. An early draft of the paper was also presented at the Workshop for PhD students on scientific work in nonprofit and philanthropy research funded by Eucor – The European Campus and held in October, 2022 in Bad Sulzburg, Germany. The essay is currently submitted at the "Social Enterprise Journal".

The second essay (*"From Social Worker to Social Entrepreneur: Dynamic Proximity in a Social Impact Incubator"*) looks into the question of how interactions and the learning process take place in a social impact incubator program. The goal of this essay was to understand the dynamics of interactions between program managers and participants. This was done through the perspective of structuration theory and the assessment of different dimensions of proximity.

The study uncovers the two essential mechanisms of proximity augmentation and proximity moderation to guide interactions in the program. On the one hand, participants were positively influenced by the program and decided to engage with actors in its environment. First, participants felt an increase in motivation and drive from having access to resources. Second, these resources were collected in the relatively short time span of the program with the intention to resort to this repository in the future. Third, not only material resources were made use of, but also virtual schemas. Participants internalized the proposed models and ways of thinking. On the other hand, participants felt that they needed to moderate their proximity to the program because of negative effects. First, many participants were hesitant to identify as social entrepreneurs. Second, they placed great importance on maintaining their previous social connections. Third, the program created demands that went beyond the capacities of some participants. In order to protect their personal well-being, they decided to moderate their proximity to the program.

These findings are congruent with the literature on innovation management and the knowledge about optimal proximity for innovation to take place (Balland et al., 2022). In this sense, proximity is optimal when neither being too great nor too low. Agents collaborating ever more closely thus is not the solution for innovative solutions to arise. Agents need to purposefully limit proximity. This is referred to as proximity paradox (Boschma & Frenken, 2010). For example, in order to be able to learn mutually, knowledge should be congruent to a certain degree but not be identical.

The second essay was presented in the European Research Network on Philanthropy (ERNOP) conference in June of 2022 in Zagreb, Croatia. The essay is currently submitted at the journal "Human Service Organizations: Management, Leadership & Governance". It is under review for the special issue "Social Innovation, Social Enterprise, Social Entrepreneurship in Social Work and Human Services".

The third essay (*"Revenue Streams of Social Impact Incubators and Accelerators: The Influence of Program Benefits"*) investigates the funding of SIIAs. The aim of this study was to understand the influence that the specific program benefits have on funding. We looked into earned, donation and government income as the most important sources of funding for SIIAs. In addition to funding, the relationship between social and economic benefits is investigated.

The results of essay three indicate that there are significant influences of the type of program benefits on funding sources. Particularly in regards to social benefits, there is a significant positive influence on higher shares of donation income and lower shares of earned income. Further, programs with economic benefits are funded by higher shares of government income. Economic benefits are associated with economic development. Thus, these SIIAs provide public benefits that are most likely to be funded by government income (Clausen & Rasmussen, 2011; Mian et al., 2016). In addition, programs with economic benefits will also be funded by lower shares of donation income. Overall, these findings are congruent with benefits theory and speak to a general alignment of the nature of benefits with funding sources.

In addition, we also hypothesized the nature of organizational hybridity in SIIAs to be characterized by tensions between social and economic aspects. The data confirm this. Higher focus on economic organizational identity of program participants influences program participants' attention to social goals negatively. Thus, the assessment of the nature of hybridity unveils a continuum of social and economic aspects in this specific context. On this continuum, an increase of economic aspects in the organizations leads to a decrease of the social and vice versa. The basic idea for this essay was presented at the PhD workshop of European Research Network on Philanthropy (ERNOP) conference in June of 2022 in Zagreb, Croatia. Further, the essay was presented at the Economics Lunch at the Faculty of Business and Economics at the University of Basel in March 2024. The essay is also scheduled to be presented at the ISTR conference in July 2024 in Antwerpen, Belgium. The essay is currently submitted at the journal "Nonprofit and Voluntary Sector Quarterly".

Title (abbr.)	Research Questions	Theories & Concepts	Method	Data
A Framework for Managing Hybridity	• What are the general statistics of the literature on management in SEs? • What are the scholarly research orientations in the field of hybridity management among SEs? • How can SEs systematically manage hybridity?	Organizational Hybridity	Systematic Literature Review	82 peer-reviewed journal articles
From Social Worker to Social Entrepreneur	• How do interactions and the learning process take place in social impact incubator programs?	Structuration Theory / Proximity	Longitudinal Single Case Study	15 semi-structured interviews, participant observation and documentation
Revenue Streams of Social Impact Incubators and Accelerators	• How do the benefits provided by social impact incubators and accelerators affect the composition of their revenue sources?	Organizational Hybridity / Benefits Theory of Nonprofit Finance	Partial Least Squares Structural Equation Model	Survey data from a questionnaire ($n = 89$)

Table 2: Overview of the three essays comprising this thesis

Critical Assessment

This thesis contributes to the knowledge on newer forms of organizations that are becoming increasingly relevant and numerous: hybrid organizations at the intersection of social impact and economic value creation. Social enterprises are the most well-known example of this type of organization. A major contribution of this thesis lies in organizing the recent literature on the management of hybridity in social enterprises. However, the landscape is diverse. In particular, there has been a rise in support and intermediary organizations for social enterprises. SIIAs belong to this category. The community that is forming around impact is global and shares a common language to some degree. However, SIIAs are diverse and little is understood about how they operate. This thesis investigates SIIAs through empirical research and sheds light on their practices. In the plethora of differences, I find principles that apply broadly to all SIIAs.

These contributions largely concern program management and financial management. The following sections elaborate on the contributions of this thesis, its practical implications, limitations and opportunities for future research.

Contributions

This thesis' main contribution lies in the investigation of the nature of hybridity in social enterprises, as well as SIIAs. Scholars are increasingly careful to put all social enterprises into the same box. This increased understanding of hybrid organizations is important for understanding founding processes and motives, as well as innovative managerial strategies. The initial academic endeavors in the realms of social entrepreneurship, social enterprise and social innovation literature have primarily centered on delineating defining characteristics (Mair & Martí, 2006). This thesis is less concerned with definitional aspects and moves the field forward by identifying practically relevant managerial strategies. In conducting quantitative empirical research, it also contributes to the lack of quantitative studies in these fields.

The contribution of essay one lies in differentiating managerial approaches with regard to degrees of hybridity in social enterprises. Previous reviews have been conducted on the strategies that are applied to manage hybridity (Battilana & Lee, 2014; Smith et al., 2013), but a conceptual basis and aggregation of the results has been lacking. Essay one contributes to the literature by basing the findings on the framework by Shepherd et al. (2019). Through the perspective of this framework, social enterprises are able to take into consideration the intensity of either logic, as well as their relative hybridity.

Essay two differentiates degrees of hybridity through the perspective of proximity. In particular, variations in the degree of hybridity of incubator program participants to the incubator environment are analyzed. Previously, proximity has mostly been studied in a spatial dimension in the literature on social innovation (Gerli et al., 2022; Tricarico et al., 2022). This study applied different dimensions of proximity, namely cognitive, social, institutional and spatial, to assess the variations in the degree of hybridity between participants and incubator environment. Essay two also contributes to the literature by uncovering implications of proximity paradox in the context of SIIAs. The dynamic augmentation and moderation of proximity to the incubator program emerges as a central mechanism. This dynamic approach to proximity research has been called for in the literature (Balland et al., 2015). In addition, a contribution lies in the application of structuration theory to contexts of social innovation dissemination (Cajaiba-Santana, 2014). Thus, I also contribute to structuration theory and proximity research by combining them. This combination proved to be a fruitful theoretical framework for the investigation and can be applied to other research areas.

In essay three, different natures of hybridity of program participants in SIIAs are investigated quantitatively. First, we contribute by gathering descriptive statistics on the landscape of SIIAs. SIIAs are a newer phenomenon, thus, little is known about how they operate (Kher et al., 2022). Second, we assess their nature of hybridity through the program participants' economic organizational identity and attention to social goals of program participants. We show that the nature of hybridity is related to the specific funding sources. This is a timely contribution when there is increasingly more research into the nexus of impact investing and social innovation research (Olson et al., 2024). Through this investigation of hybridity in SIIAs, this thesis builds theory. It contributes not only to the literature on organizational hybridity but also benefits theory. This thesis expands benefits theory to hybrid contexts at the intersection of social and economic value creation. Thus, the results of this thesis provide further empirical evidence for benefits theory.

Practical Implications

This thesis provides several implications for actors and organizations that aim to disseminate social innovations. Managing multiple objectives is one of the main demands that arise in this pursuit. Essay one organizes the findings of scholarly research of hybridity management in social enterprises in a framework. This framework can guide practitioners in improving the management of hybridity. By paying attention to the three central areas of hybridity management in the framework, all aspects that are specific to social enterprises are outlined. First, an organization needs to consider the importance of social and economic aspects relative to each other. A higher prioritization of social aspects might mean that an organization forgoes growth. On the other hand, a prioritization of economic aspects might mean that an organization will change or abandon their social mission when organizational survival is threatened. Further, many social enterprises will separate the creation of social value from economic value in a differentiated approach. Others choose an integrated approach where social value is created through the sale of a product or service directly. Second, there need to be guardrails in social enterprises that assure that neither social nor economic objectives can be dispensed with too easily. An SE that prioritizes economic aspects and organizational resilience to beneficiary impact needs to take care to impose guardrails for the social mission in order not to risk mission drift. This also means measuring each objective. In organizations, in which aspects are regarded as equally important, guardrails are not needed to the same degree. Third, a clear vision for the future needs to guide individual employees in the organization.

Essays two and three investigate management in SIIAs. This thesis has practical implications for two major areas of SIIA management: the management of incubation and acceleration programs, as well as financial management. First, incubation and acceleration programs should be structured in a way that takes into consideration the nature and characteristics of program participants. For example, it was uncovered that SIIA programs are able to change participants' knowledge structures, and thus, their view of the world. It is important to recognize that some participants will integrate faster in hybrid contexts than others. The speed and willingness of integration with the SIIA environment is determined by for example the background of participants. It is reasonable not to allow for excessive heterogeneity between participants in order to maximize learning. Too many knowledge gaps will increase difficulties to progress. However, some diversity is needed in order to promote creativity. In addition, spatial proximity should not be neglected either. The regular presence of participants in the incubator environment will support the learning process. Second, this thesis has identified important relationships between potential funders for SIIAs depending on the nature of their program participants. On the one hand, SIIAs with economically oriented program participants are best off when targeting government income. Previous literature also already indicated that governments fund SIIAs for the public benefits of economic development (Clausen & Rasmussen, 2011). On the other hand, SIIAs that provide their programs for social oriented program participants, donation income is the major funding source to target.

Limitations and Opportunities for Future Research

Despite incorporating a rather large variation of SEs and SIIAs and their differences in the nature of hybridity, this thesis does not capture degrees of hybridity in hybrid organizations other than social enterprises and SIIAs. For example, corporate foundations also operate at the intersection of social and economic aspects and they face tensions that could inform successful management of hybridity (Gehringer, 2021). Future research should assess strategies of hybridity in corporate foundations. It is expected that many strategies used in SEs can be applied, but not all. The specificities of other organizations certainly need to be investigated separately.

This thesis provides a first assessment as to which funding sources are relevant for SIIAs depending on their social and economic orientation. However, this is only a first insight into how

SIIAs are funded. Further determinants of receiving government, donation or earned income remain to be unveiled. Regarding program management, further investigation into the effect of SIIA programs on participants should be assessed. In addition, management in SIIAs does not only concern identifying funding sources and program management. For example, SIIAs need to strengthen their position as intermediaries and facilitators of networks. Future research should investigate their influence on policy-making in particular.

This thesis makes significant advances in developing the understanding of the impact that SIIA programs have on society. However, the quantitative assessments of this impact is difficult. Social impact measurement in individual SIIAs and on the SIIA landscape generally is not developed far enough. Hence, the development of evaluation methodologies should be further developed. However, scholars have worked towards an improved quantitative assessment of organizational hybridity (Shepherd et al., 2019). Measurement scales such as the logic multiplicity framework have been developed (Besharov & Smith, 2014). Further investigations into different degrees of hybridity are warranted.

In addition, this thesis focuses on social and economic aspects only. Many studies and models consider environmental aspects separately to social aspects (Longoni & Cagliano, 2018; Pellegrini et al., 2020). There are practical advantages for separately measuring negative externalities in organizations leading to environmental pollution, for example in terms of CO_2 emissions. Thus, future research should take into consideration dimensions besides social and economic aspects.

References

Abas, N., Kalair, A., & Khan, N. (2015). Review of fossil fuels and future energy technologies. *Futures*, *69*, 31-49.

Akemu, O., Whiteman, G., & Kennedy, S. (2016). Social Enterprise Emergence from Social Movement Activism: The Fairphone Case. *Journal of Management Studies*, *53*(5), 846-877.

Alberti, F. G., & Varon Garrido, M. A. (2017). Can profit and sustainability goals co-exist? New business models for hybrid firms. *Journal of Business Strategy*, *38*(1), 3-13.

Ashforth, B. E., & Reingen, P. H. (2014). Functions of Dysfunction: Managing the Dynamics of an Organizational Duality in a Natural Food Cooperative. *Administrative Science Quarterly*, *59*(3), 474-516.

Audretsch, D. B., Eichler, G. M., & Schwarz, E. J. (2021). Emerging needs of social innovators and social innovation ecosystems. *International Entrepreneurship and Management Journal*.

Balland, P.-A., Boschma, R., & Frenken, K. (2015). Proximity and Innovation: From Statics to Dynamics. *Regional Studies*, *49*(6), 907-920.

Balland, P.-A., Boschma, R., & Frenken, K. (2022). Proximity, innovation and networks: a concise review and some next steps. In *Handbook of Proximity Relations*. Cheltenham, UK: Edward Elgar Publishing.

Battilana, J., Besharov, M. L., & Mitzinneck, B. C. (2017). On hybrids and hybrid organizing: A review and roadmap for future research.

Battilana, J., & Lee, M. (2014). Advancing Research on Hybrid Organizing - Insights from the Study of Social Enterprises. *Academy of Management Annals*, *8*(1), 397-441.

Battilana, J., Sengul, M., Pache, A.-C., & Model, J. (2015). Harnessing Productive Tensions in Hybrid Organizations: The Case of Work Integration Social Enterprises. *Academy of Management Journal*, *58*(6), 1658-1685.

Bengtsson, M. (2016). How to plan and perform a qualitative study using content analysis. *NursingPlus Open*, *2*, 8-14.

Besharov, M. L., & Smith, W. K. (2014). Multiple Institutional Logics in Organizations: Explaining Their Varied Nature and Implications. *Academy of Management Review*, *39*(3), 364-381.

Bethmann, S. (2020). *Stiftungen und soziale Innovationen*. Wiesbaden: Springer.

BFS. (2023). *Entwicklung der Gesundheitsausgaben*. Bundesamt für Statistik. Retrieved 23 February from https://www.bfs.admin.ch/bfs/de/home/statistiken/querschnittsthemen/wohlfahrtsmess ung/alle-indikatoren/gesellschaft/gesundheitsausgaben.html

Boschma, R. (2005). Proximity and Innovation: A Critical Assessment. *Regional Studies*, *39*(1), 61-74.

Boschma, R., & Frenken, K. (2010). The spatial evolution of innovation networks: a proximity perspective. In *The handbook of evolutionary economic geography*. Edward Elgar Publishing.

Bruneel, J., Clarysse, B., Weemaes, S., & Staessens, M. (2020). Breaking With the Past: The Need for Innovation in the Governance of Nonprofit Social Enterprises. *Academy of Management Perspectives*, *34*(2), 209-225.

Cajaiba-Santana, G. (2010). Socially constructed opportunities in social entrepreneurship: a structuration model. In *Handbook of Research on Social Entrepreneurship* (pp. 88-106). Cheltenham, UK: Edward Elgar Publishing.

Cajaiba-Santana, G. (2014). Social innovation: Moving the field forward. A conceptual framework. *Technological Forecasting and Social Change*, *82*, 42-51.

Chen, X., & Kelly, T. F. (2015). B-Corps—A Growing Form of Social Enterprise:Tracing Their Progress and Assessing Their Performance. *Journal of Leadership & Organizational Studies*, *22*(1), 102-114.

Clausen, T., & Rasmussen, E. (2011). Open innovation policy through intermediaries: the industry incubator programme in Norway. *Technology Analysis & Strategic Management*, *23*(1), 75-85.

Cornelissen, J. P., Akemu, O., Jonkman, J. G. F., & Werner, M. D. (2021). Building Character: The Formation of a Hybrid Organizational Identity in a Social Enterprise. *Journal of Management Studies*, *58*(5), 1294-1330.

Cornforth, C. (2014). Understanding and combating mission drift in social enterprises. *Social Enterprise Journal*, *10*(1), 3-20.

Domanski, D., Howaldt, J., & Kaletka, C. (2019). A comprehensive concept of social innovation and its implications for the local context – on the growing importance of social innovation ecosystems and infrastructures. *European Planning Studies*, *28*, 1-21.

Dufays, F. (2019). Exploring the drivers of tensions in social innovation management in the context of social entrepreneurial teams. *Management Decision*, *57*(6), 1344-1361.

Dupain, W., Scharpe, K., Gazeley, T., Bennett, T., Mair, J., Raith, M., & Bosma, N. (2022). *The State of Social Enterprise in Europe – European Social Enterprise Monitor 2021-2022*. E. Network.

Ebrahim, A., Battilana, J., & Mair, J. (2014). The governance of social enterprises: Mission drift and accountability challenges in hybrid organizations. *Research in Organizational Behavior*, *34*, 81-100.

European Commission. (2021). *Social Economy Action Plan*. Retrieved 27 February 2024 from https://ec.europa.eu/social/main.jsp?catId=1537&langId=en

Fresco, L. O. (2009). Challenges for food system adaptation today and tomorrow. *Environmental Science & Policy*, *12*(4), 378-385.

Gehringer, T. (2021). Corporate Foundations as Hybrid Organizations: A Systematic Review of Literature. *VOLUNTAS: International Journal of Voluntary and Nonprofit Organizations*, *32*(2), 257-275.

Gerli, F., Calderini, M., & Chiodo, V. (2022). An ecosystemic model for the technological development of social entrepreneurship: exploring clusters of social innovation. *European Planning Studies*, *30*(10), 1962-1984.

Gibbons, J., & Hazy, J. K. (2017). Leading a Large-Scale Distributed Social Enterprise: How the Leadership Culture at Goodwill Industries Creates and Distributes Value in Communities. *Nonprofit Management & Leadership*, *27*(3), 299-316.

Giddens, A. (1986). *The constitution of society: Outline of the theory of structuration*. Cambridge: Polity.

Gioia, D. (2021). A Systematic Methodology for Doing Qualitative Research. *The Journal of Applied Behavioral Science*, *57*(1), 20-29.

Gioia, D. A., Corley, K. G., & Hamilton, A. L. (2013). Seeking Qualitative Rigor in Inductive Research: Notes on the Gioia Methodology. *Organizational Research Methods*, *16*(1), 15-31.

Haigh, N., & Hoffman, A. J. (2014). The New Heretics: Hybrid Organizations and the Challenges They Present to Corporate Sustainability. *Organization & Environment*, *27*(3), 223-241.

Hersberger-Langloh, S. E., Stühlinger, S., & von Schnurbein, G. (2021). Institutional isomorphism and nonprofit managerialism: For better or worse? *Nonprofit Management and Leadership*, *31*(3), 461-480.

Hirschmann, M., Moritz, A., & Block, J. H. (2021). Motives, Supporting Activities, and Selection Criteria of Social Impact Incubators: An Experimental Conjoint Study. *Nonprofit and Voluntary Sector Quarterly*, 08997640211057402.

Howells, J. (2006). Intermediation and the role of intermediaries in innovation. *Research Policy*, *35*(5), 715-728.

Humbel, C., & Wittkämpfer, T. (2024). *Corporate Philanthropy und Sozialunternehmertum im Schweizer Unternehmensrecht*. Zurich: Dike Verlag.

Jin, B. (2020). The Practical Intelligence of Social Entrepreneurs: Managing the Hybridity of Social Enterprises. *Entrepreneurship Research Journal*, *10*(1), 19, Article 20180007.

Joseph, J., Borland, H., Orlitzky, M., & Lindgreen, A. (2020). Seeing Versus Doing: How Businesses Manage Tensions in Pursuit of Sustainability. *Journal of Business Ethics*, *164*(2), 349-370.

Kannothra, C. G., Manning, S., & Haigh, N. (2018). How Hybrids Manage Growth and Social-Business Tensions in Global Supply Chains: The Case of Impact Sourcing. *Journal of Business Ethics*, *148*(2), 271-290.

Kerlin, J. A., Lall, S. A., Peng, S., & Cui, T. S. (2021). Institutional intermediaries as legitimizing agents for social enterprise in China and India. *Public Management Review*, *23*(5), 731-753.

Kher, R., Yang, S., & Newbert, S. L. (2022). Accelerating emergence: the causal (but contextual) effect of social impact accelerators on nascent for-profit social ventures. *Small Business Economics*.

Knutsson, H., & Thomasson, A. (2017). Exploring organisational hybridity from a learning perspective. *Qualitative Research in Accounting & Management*, *14*(4), 430-447.

Krippendorff, K. (2004). *Content Analysis: An Introduction to Its Methodology* (2nd ed.). Thousand Oaks, CA: Sage Publications.

Kurland, N. B., & Schneper, W. D. (2021). A Social Enterprise's Hybridising Journey to Reconcile Goals and Structure with Identity. *Journal of Social Entrepreneurship*, 1-26.

Lall, S. A., Chen, L.-W., & Roberts, P. W. (2020). Are we accelerating equity investment into impact-oriented ventures? *World Development*, *131*, 104952.

Longoni, A., & Cagliano, R. (2018). Sustainable Innovativeness and the Triple Bottom Line: The Role of Organizational Time Perspective. *Journal of Business Ethics*, *151*(4), 1097-1120.

Mair, J., & Martí, I. (2006). Social entrepreneurship research: A source of explanation, prediction, and delight. *Journal of World Business*, *41*(1), 36-44.

Mian, S., Lamine, W., & Fayolle, A. (2016). Technology Business Incubation: An overview of the state of knowledge. *Technovation*, *50-51*, 1-12.

Mulgan, G. (2006). The process of social innovation. *MIT Press*, *1*, 145-162.

Murray, R., Caulier-Grice, J., & Mulgan, G. (2010). *The Open Book of Social Innovation*. London: NESTA.

Ocasio, W. (1997). Towards an Attention-Based View of the Firm. *Strategic Management Journal*, *18*, 187-206.

Olson, H., Painter, G., Albertson, K., Fox, C., & O'Leary, C. (2024). Are Social Impact Bonds an Innovation in Finance or Do They Help Finance Social Innovation? *Journal of Social Policy*, *53*(2), 407-431.

Pandey, S., Lall, S., Pandey, S. K., & Ahlawat, S. (2017). The Appeal of Social Accelerators: What do Social Entrepreneurs Value? *Journal of Social Entrepreneurship*, *8*(1), 88-109.

Pellegrini, G., Annosi, M. C., Conto, F., & Fiore, M. (2020). What Are the Conflicting Tensions in an Italian Cooperative and How Do Members Manage Them? Business Goals', Integrated Management, and Reduction of Waste within a Fruit and Vegetables Supply Chain. *Sustainability*, *12*(7), 15, Article 3050.

Saebi, T., Foss, N. J., & Linder, S. (2019). Social Entrepreneurship Research: Past Achievements and Future Promises. *Journal of Management*, *45*(1), 70-95.

Sanzo-Pérez, M. J., Rey-García, M., & Álvarez-González, L. I. (2021). Downward accountability to beneficiaries in social enterprises: do partnerships with nonprofits boost it without undermining accountability to other stakeholders? *Review of Managerial Science*.

Sarason, Y., Dean, T., & Dillard, J. F. (2006). Entrepreneurship as the nexus of individual and opportunity: A structuration view. *Journal of Business Venturing, 21*(3), 286-305.

Sarhangi, R., Mashayekhi, A. N., & Souzanchi Kashani, E. (2021). From Black and White to Yin and Yang: Exploring the Management of Tensions in Social Enterprises. *Journal of Social Entrepreneurship*, 1-25.

Sarma, S. K. (2020). Retaining the social goal: role of path creation in for-profit social enterprises. *Journal of Management History, 26*(1), 77-98.

Sewell, W. H. (1992). A Theory of Structure: Duality, Agency, and Transformation. *American Journal of Sociology, 98*(1), 1-29.

Shepherd, D. A., Williams, T. A., & Zhao, E. Y. (2019). A Framework for Exploring the Degree of Hybridity in Entrepreneurship. *Academy of Management Perspectives, 33*(4), 491-512.

Siebold, N., Gunzel-Jensen, F., & Muller, S. (2019). Balancing dual missions for social venture growth: a comparative case study. *Entrepreneurship and Regional Development, 31*(9-10), 710-734.

Siegner, M., Pinkse, J., & Panwar, R. (2018). Managing tensions in a social enterprise: The complex balancing act to deliver a multi-faceted but coherent social mission. *Journal of Cleaner Production, 174*, 1314-1324.

Smith, W. K., & Besharov, M. L. (2019). Bowing before Dual Gods: How Structured Flexibility Sustains Organizational Hybridity. *Administrative Science Quarterly, 64*(1), 1-44.

Smith, W. K., Gonin, M., & Besharov, M. L. (2013). Managing Social-Business Tensions: A Review and Research Agenda for Social Enterprise. *Business Ethics Quarterly, 23*(3), 407-442.

Stevens, R., Moray, N., & Bruneel, J. (2015). The Social and Economic Mission of Social Enterprises: Dimensions, Measurement, Validation, and Relation. *Entrepreneurship Theory and Practice, 39*(5), 1051-1082.

Teasdale, S. (2012). Negotiating Tensions: How Do Social Enterprises in the Homelessness Field Balance Social and Commercial Considerations? *Housing Studies, 27*(4), 514-532.

Timulak, L. (2009). Meta-analysis of qualitative studies: A tool for reviewing qualitative research findings in psychotherapy. *Psychotherapy Research, 19*(4-5), 591-600.

Timulak, L. (2014). Qualitative Meta-Analysis. In *The SAGE Handbook of Qualitative Data Analysis* (pp. 481-495). SAGE Publications Ltd

Tricarico, L., De Vidovich, L., & Billi, A. (2022). Entrepreneurship, inclusion or co-production? An attempt to assess territorial elements in social innovation literature. *Cities, 130*, 103986.

Voltan, A., & De Fuentes, C. (2016). Managing multiple logics in partnerships for scaling social innovation. *European Journal of Innovation Management, 19*(4), 446-467.

Yin, J. L., & Chen, H. (2019). Dual-goal management in social enterprises: evidence from China. *Management Decision, 57*(6), 1362-1381.

Young, D. R. (2017). *Financing Nonprofits and Other Social Enterprises: A Benefits Approach*. Cheltenham, UK: Edward Elgar Publishing.

Essay One

A Framework for Managing Hybridity in Social Enterprises

Lucca Nietlispach

Abstract

Social enterprises (SEs) aim to achieve dual missions through hybrid organizing. Research on the strategies for managing hybridity is growing, although a systematic conceptualization of the most recent findings is lacking. A comprehensive framework for the management of hybridity involving the joint pursuit of social and economic goals is warranted. This article builds such a framework through a systematic literature review of a sample of 82 articles published in peer-reviewed journals. Hybridity is often conceptualized through a continuum approach, in which there is a strong social logic on one end of the continuum and a strong economic logic on the other. This paper extends this approach by examining different degrees of hybridity. By classifying managerial strategies into three fundamental categories, the recent literature on hybridity and SEs are organized into a theory-driven framework. Additionally, practitioners in SEs and other organizations have a comprehensive overview of the strategies used to manage hybridity. These findings are also relevant to nonprofit organizations facing marketization pressure and private companies aiming to incorporate social goals into their profit-generating activities.

Keywords: organizational hybridity, social enterprise, social entrepreneurship, degrees of hybridity, strategy, management

Introduction

Social entrepreneurship is widely acknowledged as a promising tool for achieving system change and addressing urgent social and environmental issues. Social entrepreneurship has been broadly defined as "individuals, organizations, or initiatives engaged in entrepreneurial activities with a social goal" (Bacq et al., 2013, p. 40). Early social entrepreneurship research was characterized by attempts to define the field more clearly (Chell, 2007; Weerawardena & Mort, 2006) and delineate the boundaries of commercial entrepreneurship (Austin et al., 2006; Lumpkin et al., 2013). Currently, many ambiguities in the definition of social entrepreneurship remain (Morris et al., 2020), but scholars have not held back in researching the phenomenon because of its increasing relevance in practice. The author agrees with Mair and Martí (2006) that these ambiguities present an opportunity for advancing management research. One of the central research topics in social entrepreneurship is related to a combination of nonprofit and business sector aspects and the resulting hybridity of social and economic logics.

Whereas social entrepreneurship is an essentially human-centered and agency-related concept due to its focus on entrepreneurial individuals, social enterprise (SE) research is focused on the organizational form (Westley & McConnell, 2010). Hybridity is a defining trait of SEs. Management in hybrid SEs is different from that in nonprofit organizations and private companies in various ways. Like businesses, hybrids strive for growth, but ever-increasing market share is not their central goal due to the possible negative effects that this might exert on the social mission. Additionally, social systems are internalized and not regarded as separate from the organization (Haigh & Hoffman, 2014). Conversely, hybrids also differ from nonprofit organizations in that they do not rely solely on philanthropic capital and place a focus on social problems that have a feasible market-based solution. SEs in all areas face unique challenges in determining the correct ecosystem and developing needed skills for growing the organization and overcoming resource constraints (Åstebro & Hoos, 2021). Many of these challenges are inherently related to the joint pursuit of a social and commercial mission. For example, SE leadership faces practical challenges because of the difficulty posed by setting a clear goal in advance (Schröer & Jäger, 2015; Smith et al., 2012). Prioritizing financial sustainability leads to mission drift (Grimes et al., 2019), while prioritizing the social mission can lead to a failure to cover operational costs and maintain financial independence. In combining institutional logics from the business and nonprofit sectors, social entrepreneurs must conduct what has been called "dual mission management" (Costanzo et al., 2014; Siegner et al., 2018) or "hybrid organizing" (Battilana & Lee, 2014). Even though this balancing act between their social and economic goals creates difficulties, SEs are founded on the premise that this hybridity has several beneficial aspects. Scholars have found that hybridity supports better performance (Mongelli et al., 2019) and can be conducive to growth (Davies et al., 2019). Salavou and Manolopoulos (2021) found that hybrid options, compared to pure strategic options, exert more influential impacts in terms of positive environmental, social and economic contributions. Even economic efficiency has been found to lead to greater social impact in SEs that manage to maintain balance with their social mission (Staessens et al., 2019). To harness the positive effects of hybridity, the negative consequences that result from hybridity need to be mitigated. Numerous managerial strategies incorporating multiple institutional logics have been identified in the literature. However, a systematic assessment of the most recent literature on the management of hybridity is lacking. This study aims to address this research gap. Articles with a rather exclusive focus on hybrid organizing have been published in the last several years. This recent rise in publications presents an opportunity to comprehensively assess the distinct categories of strategies for managing hybridity. Research investigating the strategies used to overcome the challenges of managing hybridity is highly relevant for better understanding the managerial processes of hybrid organizing. This systematic literature review aims to answer the following research questions:

RQ1: What is the state of the literature on management in SEs? (publications per year, publishing journals, regions investigated, research methods)

Scholars have taken different approaches to the investigation of hybridity management in SEs. The different perspectives from which this topic can be addressed lead to the following question:

RQ2: What are the scholarly research orientations in the field of hybridity management among SEs?

Taking a nuanced approach, this study also investigates the different degrees of hybridity and their implications for management strategies. Thus, the third question addressed in this paper is the following:

RQ3: How can SEs systematically manage hybridity?

By reviewing the academic literature of the last 10 years, this study advances the field by delineating the relationships among the strategies used in SEs to manage hybridity. This understanding is incorporated into a single framework.

Given the blurring of the nonprofit and for-profit sectors (Billis, 2010), managing hybridity is also becoming more important for organizations outside of SEs. For example, nonprofit organizations face marketization pressure and private companies aim to incorporate social goals into their profit-generating activities. The findings are important for several reasons. First, despite the investment of financial and other resources in nascent hybrid organizations, many of them fail, which harms different stakeholders and wastes a large portion of the invested resources. Second, emerging literature shows that balancing prosocial motivation with financial demands can be detrimental to the mental well-being of social entrepreneurs (Kibler et al., 2019). This negative effect can be mitigated through the application of appropriate management tools.

The next section describes the theoretical understanding of hybridity and subsequently details the methods of data collection and analysis used. The first part of the findings provides a descriptive overview of the analyzed literature. Furthermore, different research orientations are identified, and the framework for managing hybridity is elaborated. Before concluding, the findings are discussed, and the contributions and limitations of this study are presented.

Theoretical Background: Hybridity and Institutional Complexity

Hybridity has various applications in research. The term originated in biology (McMullen, 2018), and was later applied in the humanities and social sciences (Canclini, 2015). Within new institutional economics, hybridity refers to intraorganizational phenomena such as maintaining the dual characteristics of bureaucracy and entrepreneurship in a firm (Williamson, 1985). Only more recently has hybridity been used in organization studies to refer to organizations as a whole (Pache & Santos, 2013a).

The institutional logic approach is often taken in hybrid theory. It was developed within the wider field of institutional theory and relates to the connection between organizational form, normative frames and individual agency (Skelcher & Smith, 2015). In this view, "[o]rganizations [...] are the medium through which different logics interact with the agency of actors, and the specific dominant form of logic is historically contingent, representing the development trajectory in particular organizations" (Smith, 2014, p. 1496). In this context, hybridity is used to describe the merging of logics from different fields (Evers, 2005; Maier et al., 2014), which results in institutional complexity (Besharov & Smith, 2014). This is in contrast to modern organization theory, which proposes that organizational forms are distinct and well-bounded (Di Maggio & Powell, 1983).

There have been different types of hybrids identified in the literature (Mair et al., 2015). One perspective views hybrids as being located at the interface of sectors, such as the interface between the private and nonprofit sector. An alternative perspective is focused on variations in governance mechanisms (Seibel, 2015). Hybridity has been studied in many organizational contexts. For example, biotech firms that originated in universities tend to combine a research logic with a commercial business model (Powell & Sandholtz, 2012), while those that originated in medical education institutions tend to incorporate health care and academic logics (Dunn & Jones, 2010). The hybridity investigated in the current study of the management of hybridity in SEs lies in the combination of social and economic logics. This specific type of hybridity has been studied from both the social (Skelcher & Smith, 2015) and economic (Haigh & Hoffman, 2012) perspectives.

Many organizations adopt hybridity at a later stage in their organizational life. Conversely, SEs were founded as hybrid organizations. They are referred to by Billis (2010) as organic and enacted hybrids. Research on SEs has focused largely on organizational hybridity because hybridity is these organizations' defining trait (Hoffman et al., 2012). Even though there are other organizations that are defined by hybridity, such as corporate foundations (Gehringer, 2021), SEs have been deemed an ideal type of hybrid organization (Battilana & Lee, 2014). The term "hybrid organization" has been used as a replacement for "social enterprise" in some areas (Alberti & Varon Garrido, 2017; Haigh & Hoffman, 2014). The rest of this section will introduce a conceptual basis for understanding the nature of hybridity in SEs.

In the continuum approach, the social and economic logics of SEs are conceptualized along a spectrum (Dees, 1998) with a strong social logic on one end, and a strong economic logic on the other (Battilana et al., 2017). A balanced approach lies in between these two steps. Several scholars have investigated possible extensions of this approach (Hahn, 2020). For example, Besharov and Smith (2014) developed the logic multiplicity framework that conceptualizes the different degrees of hybridity according to the centrality and compatibility of logics. Degrees of hybridity are not limited to only two dimensions, however. Kannampuzha and Hockerts (2019) developed a scale composed of three dimensions.

This study focuses on the framework of Shepherd et al. (2019). These researchers assessed hybridity in two dimensions, namely, logic intensity and relative hybridity (Figure 2). On the one hand, the intensity of social and economic logics varies between organizations. It can range from weak to strong for either dimension. While a small family business engaged in the local community is characterized by the low intensity of both mission orientations, a SE exhibiting economic growth and expansion of its social mission is characterized by high intensity of both its social and economic missions (Shepherd et al., 2019). On the other hand, there is also variation in the degree of relative hybridity. Relative hybridity relates to the relative importance of the social and economic logics in hybrid organizations. For example, a classic for-profit organization with minor CSR activities exhibits low relative hybridity because the economic logic is significantly more important than the social logic. A nonprofit organization generating a small portion of its revenue as earned income also exhibits low relative hybridity because of the lack of importance of the economic logic. Both cases exhibit the same low degree of hybridity, but the relationship between the intensity of the social and economic logics is reversed.

Figuratively, an organization with high relative hybridity is positioned on or around the diagonal in a coordinate system in which social and economic logics serve as the axes (Figure 2). Hence, the relativity of logics can be measured by shifts on the curves of the same degree of hybridity, while an increase in overall intensity is indicated by a shift of the curve. An increase in either logic intensity or relative hybridity can lead to a greater degree of hybridity (Figure 2).

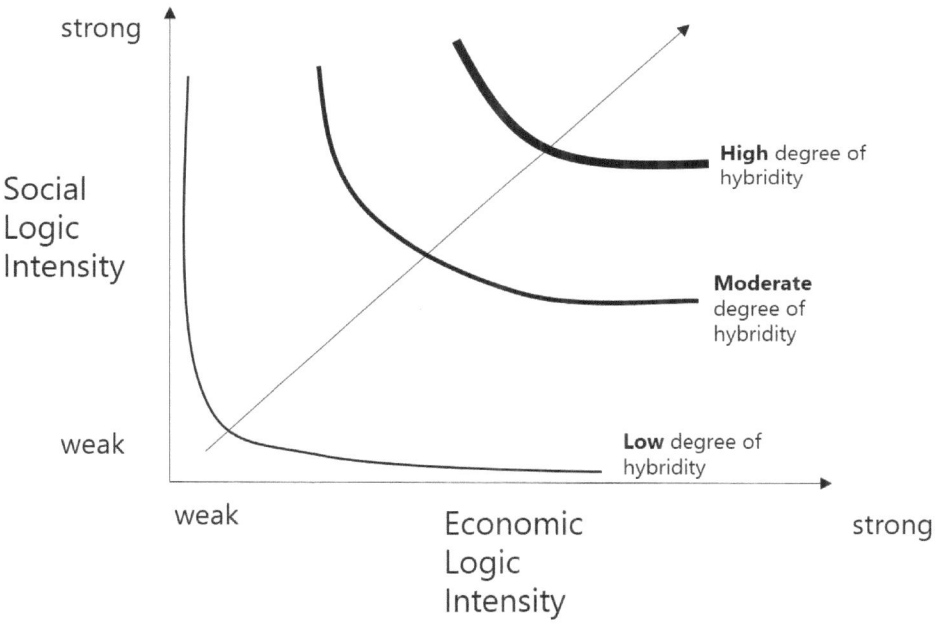

Figure 2: Different degrees of hybridity (based on Shepherd et al., 2019)

Method

This literature review was conducted as a systematic review. Systematic literature reviews were first used in the medical sciences but have since been widely adopted in the social sciences (Tranfield et al., 2003). In comparison to other review types, a systematic review is characterized by the use of a replicable and transparent process (Mallett et al., 2012). The goal is to identify all relevant articles, thereby minimizing bias in the response to a specific research question (Petticrew & Roberts, 2006). By bridging separate research streams, new conclusions can be drawn, and opportunities for future research can be described.

Data Collection

Articles were identified through database searches of the Web of Science and Scopus. These databases were selected due to their broad range of available peer-reviewed journals. Other assessed databases produced many irrelevant results and thus were not included. From the research question, three main concepts needing to be covered were identified: SE, hybridity and management. The relevant search terms used to cover the central concepts were identified through a preliminary review of the literature. The following search string was applied:

"social enterprise" OR "social entrepreneur*" OR "social venture" OR "social business"
AND
"hybridity" OR "hybrid"
AND
"manage*" OR "governance" OR "strateg*" OR "leadership"

Asterisks were used where they were deemed helpful for retrieving results from similar terms and alterations. The Web of Science was searched on August 5th 2021, for "title", "abstract", "author keywords", and "keywords plus", which produced 251 results. Scopus was searched on August 5th 2021, for "title", "abstract", "author keywords", and "keywords plus" and produced 206 results. This resulted in a total of 457 articles from these two databases. The two lists were aggregated into a single list, and 106 duplicate articles were removed. This resulted in 351 unique articles. Furthermore, the abstracts of the articles were categorized according to the inclusion and exclusion criteria (Table 3). The participants were divided into three categories according to their inclusion status: yes, no and maybe.

Inclusion Criteria	Exclusion Criteria
All research methods	Articles published before 2012
Peer-reviewed articles	Other article types (e.g. conference papers; book chapters)
All countries	Organizations other than SEs
All research fields	Article not written in English or German
Focused on social and economic logics	Other types of hybridity (e.g. private–public)

Table 3: Inclusion and exclusion criteria

Articles from all disciplines were purposefully included in the sample to obtain results that were not limited by disciplinary or sectoral boundaries. Articles published before 2012 were not included, as the objective of this study was to capture the current state of related research and the most recent findings regarding the management of hybridity in SEs. Only three of the results from the Web of Science and eight from Scopus were excluded based on publication date. Furthermore, on the basis of the focus on peer-reviewed articles, 82 articles published as for example conference papers or book chapters were excluded. Ultimately, after reviewing their abstracts, 69 articles were included on the basis of their ability to contribute to answering the research questions posed in this paper. Thirty articles were classified in the "maybe" category. These articles were thoroughly evaluated to determine whether they should be included. Among them, five were included. This process resulted in a preliminary list of 74 articles. Through a backward snowballing technique, eleven additional articles were identified as relevant for the review and thus included in the sample (Wohlin, 2014). Seven articles were removed again during the early analysis phase because they were not deemed relevant after review. This process resulted in a final sample of 78 articles. December 31st, 2021 was defined as the final cutoff date. A total of 40 articles were identified after the first search of the databases was performed on August 5th, 2021, using the same procedure as detailed above, and six additional articles were included. Further backward snowballing did not lead to any newly identified articles. Thus, the final sample consisted of 82 articles (Figure 3).

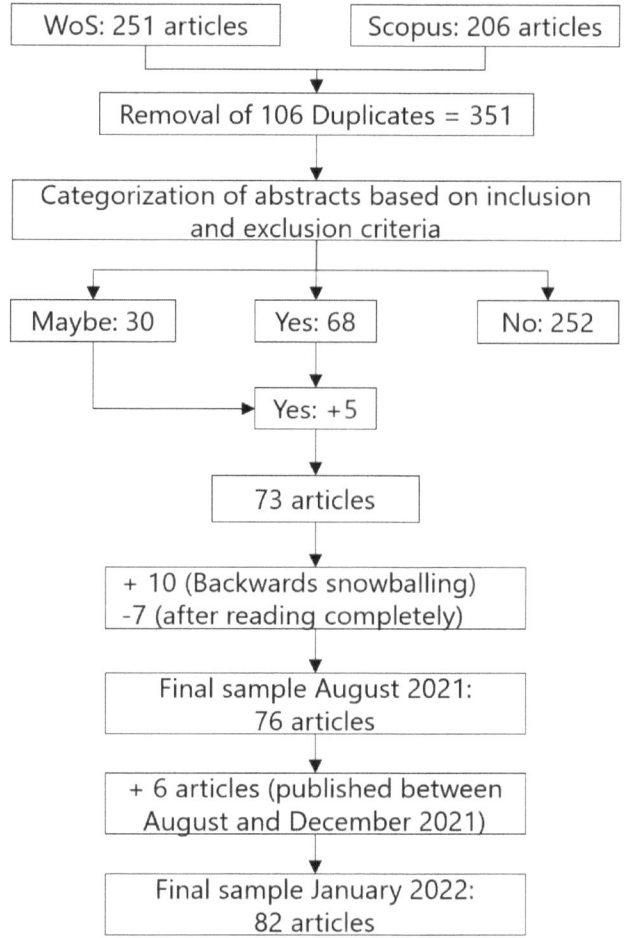

Figure 3: Literature review process (own illustration)

Data analysis

The articles were exported from the Reference Manager Endnote, and the bibliographical references, including PDF files, were imported into MAXQDA Plus 2020 (Release 20.0.8) for coding. The publication year and journal were automatically coded from the export. A sample of 25 articles was manually coded according to research method, research question and main findings. The sample was chosen such that it would be representative of the entire population in terms of publication year. In addition to the coding of the initial sample of 25 articles, further information was coded to contribute to answering the research questions (Table 4). The articles were coded via content analysis (Bengtsson, 2016). The goal of content analysis is to analyze texts by their use contexts (Krippendorff, 2004). This approach allows to quantitatively assess qualitative data, which in this case is the analyzed articles. By coding, for example, the research methods used in all the articles, conclusions can be drawn about the prevalence of empirical and theoretical research methods in the field (Figure 6). The final codes used for these 82 articles were research question, main findings, nature of tension, research orientation, research method, country of studied SE, type of SE and managerial strategy (Table 4). Three distinct types of research orientations were identified from the sample of 25 articles, namely, (1) social entrepreneurs and their skills, (2) a focus on areas of management and (3) specific guiding principles.

Aspect	Description	Categories
Research question	Coded in text	
Main findings	Coded in text	
Nature of hybridity	Coded in text	- Beneficial vs. detrimental - Process/long time frame - Multiplicity of institutional logics
Research orientation	Articles grouped as a whole	- Social entrepreneurs and their skills - Focused on a specific organizational area of management - Guiding principles
Research method	Articles grouped as a whole	- Multiple Case Study - Single Case Study - Conceptual/Theoretical - Quantitative - Other Qualitative - Mixed Methods
Country of studied SE	(Case study) articles grouped as a whole	
Type of SE	(Case study) articles grouped as a whole	
Managerial strategy	Coded in text	

Table 4: Coding framework

Furthermore, qualitative meta-analysis was applied to summarize the main findings coded in the content analysis. A qualitative meta-analysis is well suited for assessing findings across qualitative studies on the same research topic. Additionally, this approach is used to investigate the influence of the investigative method on results (Timulak, 2009). Through a holistic understanding of the article, the core ideas of the article can be categorized, described and linked to each other (Timulak, 2014). Qualitative meta-analysis allows to discover differences in a group of studies; thus, it is suited for investigating the fragmented field of hybrid organizing (Timulak, 2007).

Results

Descriptive Findings

The content analysis yielded a quantitative assessment of the sampled articles. During the ten-year time span, more than 50% of the articles were published in the final three years, which confirms the need to assess new findings and establishes the relevance of the review (Figure 4).

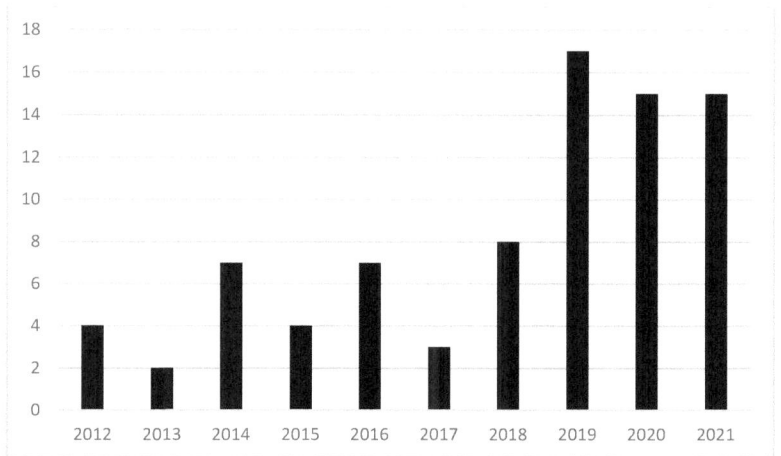

Figure 4: Number of articles published per year since 2012 (own illustration)

In the sample of 82 articles, 14 journals published two or more of the articles (Figure 5). The Journal of Business Ethics published the most studies, with a total of eight. In addition, the Social Enterprise Journal and the Journal of Social Entrepreneurship are strongly represented. Many of the publishing journals in this area publish articles on business- and management-related topics.

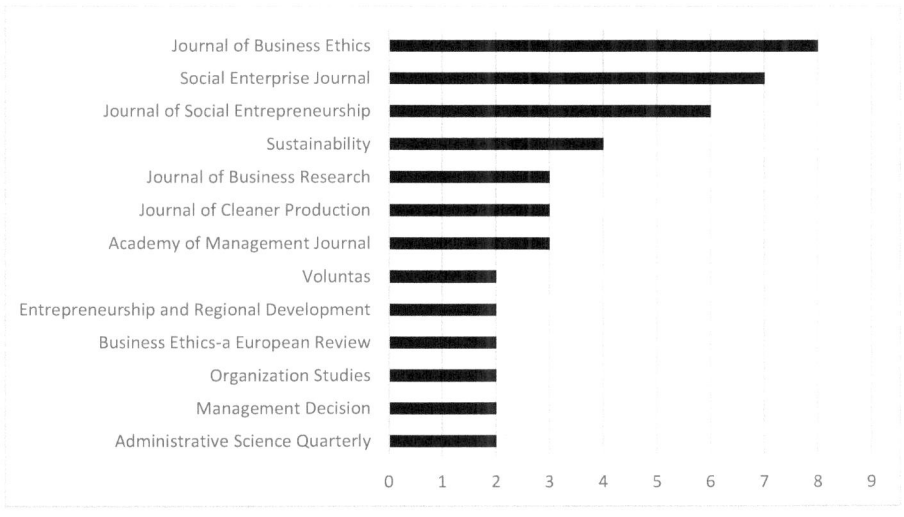

Figure 5: Journals publishing articles with more than a single citation (own illustration)

Most of the articles were qualitative or conceptual in nature (Figure 6). Single and multiple case studies have been extensively used. The regions of SEs studied in the case study articles were further evaluated. Twelve out of 35 multiple case studies focus on SEs in more than one country. SEs from every continent are represented. Of the 41 case study papers investigating SEs in a single country, 23 investigated organizations in Europe, eight in Asia, four in Africa, three in North America, two in South America and one in Australia.

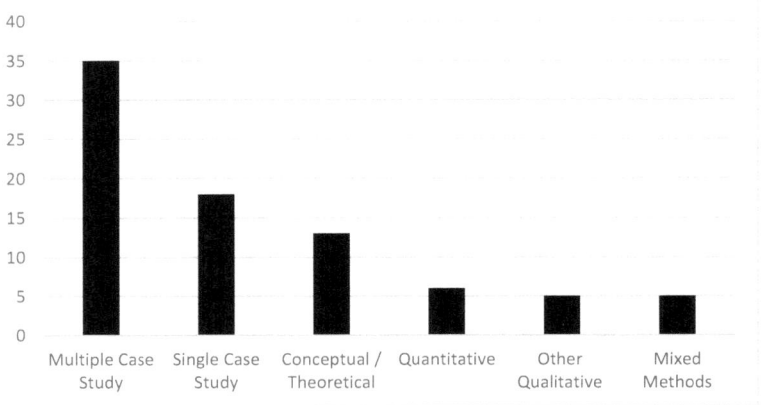

Figure 6: Research methods (own illustration)

The challenges facing SEs are often related to regional differences and the respective role of government in the area. In Europe, the European Union has made efforts to support the development of SEs (European Commission, 2021; Tykkylainen & Ritala, 2021). Some countries, such as the UK, have introduced particular legal forms for SEs (Perrini et al., 2010). Other European countries, such as Spain, support SEs through subsidies (Sanzo-Pérez et al., 2021). In Asia, the situation differs strongly depending on the country. In China, SEs are heavily dependent on the government (Yin & Chen, 2019). Hence, SEs face legitimacy challenges. While there are new legal forms that SEs can adapt in countries such as the UK or Germany (Cornforth, 2014), there is no designated legal form for SEs in China (Yin & Chen, 2019). Consequently, image management is more important for SEs in this context. In South Korea, the government is strongly involved in the support of SEs, for example, by providing tax incentives or insurance benefits (Jin, 2020). The SE Promotion Act was instituted to establish the provisioning of certification. This has significantly increased the public's recognition of SEs (Park, 2020). Stakeholder involvement and democratic governance structures are particularly important as well (Kim et al., 2020). Despite the fact that a number of studies have investigated SEs in developing countries, there is still a lack of related research. Even though the number of SEs is increasing in the global south, knowledge on SEs in the context of for example South America and Africa (Ciambotti & Pedrini, 2021) remains underdeveloped.

Furthermore, the various fields in which SEs operate have been studied. Work integration social enterprises (WISEs) (Battilana et al., 2015; Teasdale, 2012), fair trade SEs (Davies & Doherty, 2019; Mason & Doherty, 2016) and microfinance SEs (Sarma, 2020; Simatele & Dlamini, 2020) are among the most prevalent SE types. However, fields such as drug rehabilitation (Imperatori & Ruta, 2015) and agriculture (Pellegrini et al., 2020) have also been studied. The type of studied SE determines other relevant aspects that extend beyond the social and economic dimension in the specific operational context. In particular, environmental aspects also play an important role in many SEs (Pellegrini et al., 2020). Some scholars include the environmental logic in the category of the social logic. For example, Reuter (2022) investigated environmental aspects and implicitly considered them to be a subcategory of social aspects.

Thematic Findings

Research Orientations

An analysis of the literature on the management of hybridity in SEs enabled the identification of scholarly research orientations. Each research orientation is characterized by a specific scholarly focus on hybridity management in SEs. Three research orientations emerged: (1) social entrepreneurs and their skills, (2) a specific organizational management area and (3) an outline of the overarching guiding principles. These three research orientations can be viewed as perspectives for investigating strategies for managing hybridity. An understanding of these factors can help scholars situate their own approach to studying the management of hybridity. In the remainder of this section, the commonality of the articles pertaining to each research orientation is discussed.

Social entrepreneurs and their skills. The findings of a total of 26 articles are focused on individual social entrepreneurs and their skills. Social entrepreneurial ingenuity has long been a focus of research (Siegner et al., 2018). The effect of individual skills on SEs is strong throughout all stages of organizational development. However, it is particularly strong in the nascent stage of organizational activity. During this stage, the organizations' social purpose is often strongly connected to the values of the founders. During the founding process, an SE can be imprinted (Battilana et al., 2015; Sarma, 2020). By founders transferring their ethics during the building of a "caring enterprise" (André & Pache, 2016), they can exert a strong influence resulting from their emotional involvement (Ashforth & Reingen, 2014). As an SE becomes more established and legitimized, individual practical intelligence facilitates the creation of both social and economic value (Jin, 2020). The literature categorized within this research orientation shows how the skills of individual social entrepreneurs are of significant importance in the successful management of hybridity. For instance, social entrepreneurs are able to hold several frames of reference and can identify with both social and commercial values (Zur, 2020). This enables them to frame away paradoxical conditions in some cases (Child, 2020; Smith et al., 2012).

Focus on a management area. Another 24 articles investigated the management of hybridity not at the micro level of individual skills but rather through the lens of established management disciplines. This subset of the sampled articles addresses the research question through a focus on a specific management area or particular organizational aspect of the SE. With a sole focus on the individual level, it is difficult to manage hybridity because of the inherent institutional complexity involved. Entrepreneurial skills are not sufficient to manage such complexity, especially in more mature organizations. Formal structures can be implemented in an established management area to support this process. The following areas of management were explored: (1) governance and boards, (2) supply chain management, (3) stakeholder management, and (4) product management. These areas are identified as particularly important in the management of hybridity. This body of literature expands the established management disciplines through the introduction of strategies for managing hybridity. This adaptation of known theories and concepts in the context of hybrid organizations contributes to the theoretical development in the respective area.

Guiding principles. A third type of approach for researching the management of hybridity in SEs comprises articles identifying a set of guiding principles that can be used to direct organizational activities. Thirty-two articles were identified in this category. These guiding principles, or key enablers, can help a SE integrate the social and economic aspects of hybridity. These principles cover several organizational areas and connect the micro, meso and macro levels.

Striving toward the creation of coherence in organizational activities emerges as a key theme in the articles oriented toward the identification of guiding principles. Many principles support the process of translating vision into organizational practices. Such principles involve broadening the picture and understanding the relevant interrelationships. Thus, it is no surprise that nine case studies within this research orientation studied SEs across multiple fields. Furthermore, research into business models is an emerging field within the research orientation characterized by the identification of guiding principles. Applying business models to SE activities is a prototypical way of identifying guiding principles because the purpose of business models is to provide a comprehensive overview of an organization's activities (Matzembacher et al., 2020; Reuter, 2022).

Strategies

Many of the previous findings on managerial strategies for hybrid organizing are incomparable with each other, are not grounded in prior knowledge and are lacking in theoretical grounding (Sadiq et al., 2022). Thus, the aim of the analysis was not only to perform a panoramic assessment and categorization of the literature but also to create a coherent account of how the different hybridity management strategies are interrelated and how they can be integrated in a systematic fashion. The following findings extend the continuum approach to investigate different degrees of hybridity based on the framework of Shepherd et al. (2019). The conceptualization of varying degrees of hybridity provides the basis for contextualizing the findings on managerial strategies in a unified framework. The developed framework incorporates strategies for hybridity management and consists of (1) positioning regarding relative hybridity, (2) the setting of guardrails to avoid excessively low relative hybridity and (3) the efforts to increase the degree of hybridity (Figure 7).

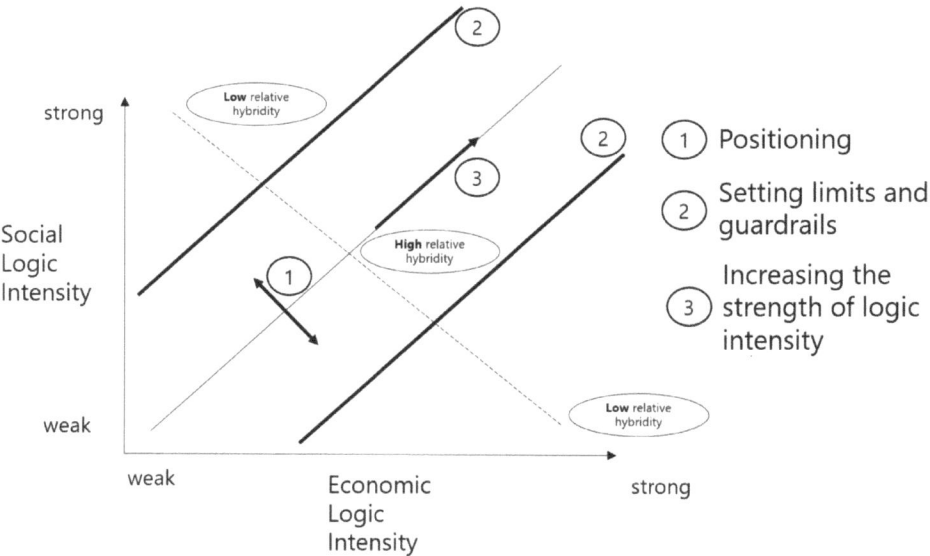

Figure 7: Framework for managing tensions (based on Shepherd et al., 2019)

Positioning

Generally, SEs have three options regarding their positions toward relative hybridity. They can prioritize commercial goals, they can prioritize social goals or they can consider both goals to be equally important. The prioritization of one goal is proclaimed by some scholars as an optimal strategy for ensuring sustainable SE operations. For example, Woodside (2018) found that WISEs that placed equal weight on these goals ultimately faced significant and unsustainable tensions. Similarly, the SEs studied by Alsaid and Ambilichu (2021) show a clear prioritization of the economic over the social mission to increase legitimacy in the eyes of the government. A dominant logic focus has implications for the development of organizational trajectories, for example, those regarding the most important stakeholders.

In contrast to organizations prioritizing one logic over the other, there are many scholars who consider equal prioritization to be the better form of hybridity management. In other words, these researchers suggest always maintaining the highest possible relative hybridity level. They warn that the prioritization of one logic and the consequent low relative hybridity level can result in conflict and might ultimately lead to irreconcilable tensions or failure (Siwale et al., 2021). Maibom and Smith (2016) found that assigning equal relative importance to both logics significantly contributes to reducing the level of institutional complexity. Similarly, Ramus et al. (2016) asserted that the importance of both logics has increased for WISEs and that they cannot overprioritize either one. This approach is more intuitive to the comprehension of SEs as an organizational form characterized by two separate core logics (Ebrahim et al., 2014). This strategic choice concerns the organizations' overall mission. However, the literature indicates that there are different levels of relative hybridity in an organization.

A distinction between the individual and organizational levels can be made. In fact, Ashforth and Reingen (2014) found that a distinct relative hybridity of logics on the individual level and on the group level is ultimately beneficial for SEs. For individuals, Ashforth and Reingen (2014) state that "[…] a compromise of this essential duality may simply negate the essence of each side, turning necessary black and white into impotent grey" (p. 506). In this case, a certain degree of dysfunctionality at the group level was shown to enable functionality at the organizational level. Thus, these authors stressed the importance of workforce diversity, as many scholars have (Powell et al., 2019). Similarly, Battilana et al. (2015) made a similar observation in examining a WISE, where "positive confrontations" at the individual level were observed to be beneficial at the organizational level. Furthermore, Maibom and Smith (2016) posited that there is a consensus among social entrepreneurs that the end justifies the mean, and therefore differences in the relative hybridity of employees become accepted by agreeing to a shared goal. This indicates that an SE workforce can and possibly should be diverse if that diversity facilitates effective conflict management and the formulation of beneficial strategies through effective leadership (Ismail & Johnson, 2019).

At both the organizational and individual levels, relative hybridity is not necessarily constant but can rather oscillate over time (Ashforth & Reingen, 2014; Mitzinneck & Besharov, 2019). Changes can take place when the influence of individual proponents of either the social or economic logic increases. Ramus et al. (2016) found that WISEs prioritized a single logic, but the financial crisis of 2008 created a need for greater relative hybridity. At the individual level, logics can oscillate along the temporal dimension. Pellegrini et al. (2020) found in their study on a cooperative that managers prioritize a single logic for a limited amount of time before shifting their focus to the opposing logic. This enables the maintenance of high relative hybridity over time. Similarly, Sarhangi et al. (2021) discovered that "managers had been circulated between the social and commercial parts" (p.14) to lower the risk of a reduction in the level of relative hybridity. Generally, practitioners in SEs have two possible choices regarding the management of hybridity: acceptance or avoidance (Figure 8).

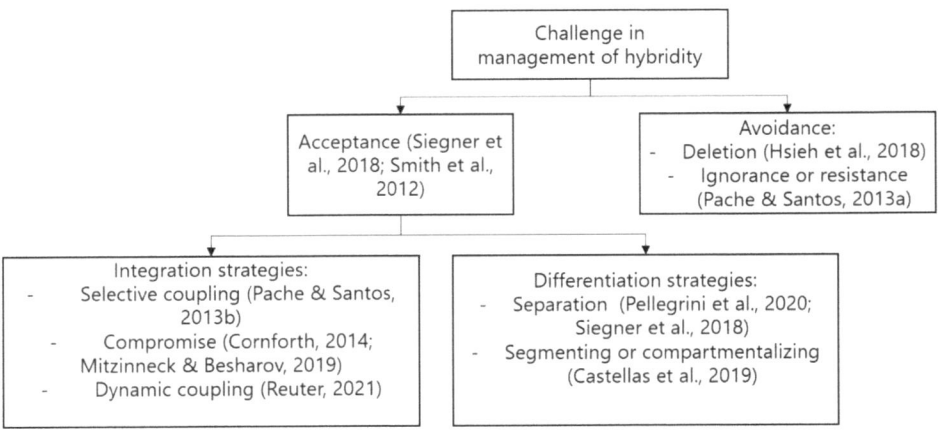

Figure 8: Strategies for managing tensions (own illustration, based on Smith et al., 2012)

Avoidance can take different forms, such as the deletion of one logic in a particular instance (Hsieh et al., 2018). This implies that either commercial or social logic is completely disregarded to resolve a problem. Furthermore, ignorance or resistance are forms of avoiding hybrid organizing (Pache & Santos, 2013a). When tensions are accepted, integration and differentiation strategies can be used to manage hybridity. Some scholars have placed acceptance on the same strategic level as integration and differentiation (Smith et al., 2012). In this study, acceptance is regarded as an antecedent of integration and differentiation strategies (Figure 8).

Integration and differentiation provide principles for structuring organizational activities. In differentiated SEs, operational areas are separate. For example, the activities that serve customers can be separated from those that serve beneficiaries (Ebrahim et al., 2014). In contrast, integrated SEs provide value through the provided product or service itself (Battilana & Lee, 2014). Integration and differentiation are broad categories, and scholars have investigated the intricacies of their applications in organizations. Pache and Santos' (2013b) seminal work on the strategy of selective coupling, which is a strategy that combines logics, reveals the mechanics of an essentially integrative strategy. They found that social entrepreneurs selectively couple intact elements of the social logic and the economic logic to create a new solution that integrates both aspects. This approach is similar to what Siebold et al. (2019) described when they proposed the process of selecting, connecting and intertwining logics. In addition, compromise is regarded as an integrative strategy (Cornforth, 2014; Mitzinneck & Besharov, 2019). The integration of the two logics requires, to some degree, an innovative and creative approach.

Strategies such as decoupling are categorized as differentiation strategies. By decoupling, operational and formal structures are separated (Pache & Santos, 2013b). Differentiation strategies require some form of bridging mechanism. This mechanism will assure that an organization maintains a high level of relative hybridity, despite the decoupling of certain aspects (Bonomi et al., 2021).

In summary, integrated SEs aim for the coherent positioning of relative hybridity throughout the organization as a whole, while differentiated SEs exhibit internal differences. Due to these differences, integration strategies are often better suited to maintaining high levels of relative hybridity, while differentiation lends itself to the prioritization of one logic and, consequently, leads to lower levels of relative hybridity. Organizations can and possibly should also oscillate between integration and differentiation strategiesover time. For example, integration and differentiation strategies can be used consecutively. For example, decoupling is a rational first reaction to tensions that are applied prior to integrative strategies, such as selective coupling, to foster a more sustainable solution (Castellas et al., 2019).

SEs with low relative hybridity must ensure that the relative importance of the dominant logic does not become overly dominant. There are limits beyond which the hybrid status of an organization has to be questioned. Managerial guardrails can help avoid transgressing these limits. The next section offers a discussion on the best ways to set up such guardrails in SEs.

Setting Guardrails

For an organization to be hybrid in nature and for SEs to be hybrid by definition, it is necessary that the level of relative hybridity not fall too low. Especially for SEs who expressly prioritize a single logic, maintaining an acceptable level of relative hybridity is critical. Guardrails impose these thresholds and enable adjustment in the case of mission drift (Smith & Besharov, 2019). Organizational guardrails refer to the creation of accountability in the decision-making process at the organizational level (Wagenschwanz & Grimes, 2021). These can be one-sided or two-sided. SEs can instate a one-sided guardrail with a focus on economic viability by, for example, making procurement decisions through a cost-benefit analysis. In this case, the guardrail consists of a financial minimum that is set, for example, at break-even (Castellas et al., 2019). Two-sided guardrails set boundaries for both missions. In this case, formal policies and metrics are used to assess not only economic viability but also social goals. Alsaid and Ambilichu (2021) particularly stress the inclusion of social metrics. However, in contrast to economic metrics, implementing social metrics is a significant challenge because a "common currency of measurement" (Ebrahim et al., 2014, p. 87) is lacking. Individual and organizational guardrails, as well as internal and external guardrails, can be differentiated.

External guardrails are often formed through stakeholder relationships (Smith & Besharov, 2019). Engaging with stakeholders such as beneficiaries creates accountability (Ramus & Vaccaro, 2017). Through social accounting, which involves the use of accountability measures such as the publication of a social impact report, a one-sided guardrail for the social mission is enacted. So-called "herding spaces" (Ometto et al., 2019) perform a similar function by facilitating interorganizational exchange and ensuring a connection to the institutional context. Furthermore, the strategy for the selection of new members for the organization can act as an external guardrail (Battilana, 2018). For example, a balanced recruitment strategy that is focused on employees from nonprofit and business organizations can reduce the danger of excessively low levels of relative hybridity.

Individual guardrails are employed by leaders in SEs (Smith & Besharov, 2019). Their expertise can reorient the trajectory of an organization in the face of difficulties. For example, one important skill of leaders is rekeying (Cornelissen et al., 2021). Rekeying refers to the act of reinterpreting understandings to create a more integrative approach. Not only the expertise of leaders but also their emotional expression can guide employees. This is achieved by, for example, reasserting confidence in times of crisis and tempering negative emotions. Emotional guardrails have most commonly been used by founders who were instrumentally identified with their organizations (Wagenschwanz & Grimes, 2021). Instrumentally identified founders of SEs rely on social conformity as the basis of their authenticity and use emotional guardrails to regulate their emotions. Founders with intrinsic identification with their organizations, however, do not need to use emotional guardrails to regulate their emotions (Wagenschwanz & Grimes, 2021). Ebrahim et al. (2014) stressed the importance of a combination of external and internal guardrails. In fact, most guardrails are focused internally and on the organizational level (Table 5). Here, it is important to create accountability for managers. Smith and Besharov (2019) use the analogies of "guardians" for each mission and situation in which one "bumps against guardrails" (p. 14). In addition, collaborative practices play an important role. In the case of conflict, solutions to emerging problems can be found in the rituals of conflict management (Ashforth & Reingen, 2014), such as negotiation spaces. Negotiation spaces are internal gatherings that allow the discussion of different perspectives within an organization (Battilana et al., 2015). In this way, the employment of people holding opposing positions regarding relative hybridity creates an overall balance (Park, 2020). The core values of employees who hold an opposing logic acts as a boundary condition (Tykkylainen & Ritala, 2021). Furthermore, collective resignation of the existing board and subsequent changes to the organization's bylaws can reorient the organization and provide a guardrail to protect against mission drift becoming too strong at the organizational level (Bruneel et al., 2020).

		Internal		External
Individual	-	Leadership expertise (Smith & Besharov, 2019)	-	Selection of members (Battilana, 2018)
	-	Rekeying (Cornelissen et al., 2021)		
	-	Emotional regulation (Wagenschwanz & Grimes, 2021)		
Organizational	-	Strategic or legal guidelines (e.g. byelaws) (Bruneel et al., 2020; Sanzo-Pérez et al., 2021)	-	Social accounting (Ramus & Vaccaro, 2017)
	-	Negotiation spaces (Battilana et al., 2015) / rituals of conflict management (Ashforth & Reingen, 2014)	-	Accountability to beneficiaries (Ebrahim et al., 2014)
	-	Board composition (Civera et al., 2020)	-	Herding spaces (Ometto et al., 2019)
	-	Accountability / monitoring of decision-making process (Ebrahim et al., 2014; Wagenschwanz & Grimes, 2021)		

Table 5: Guardrails for SEs

Increasing the Degree of Hybridity

Due to the challenges created by hybridity over a long time period, many studies have described the process of managing an increase in the degree of hybridity. There are different ways to achieve this increase. For example, such an increase can entail growth in the intensity of either logic without a decrease in the level of relative hybridity. Alternatively, an increase in relative hybridity can lead to an increase in the degree of hybridity. Both approaches facilitate mission spill-over effects. An increase in the intensity of logics can be achieved through organizational growth. Growth and the ambition to scale are central in many studies, regardless of the size and maturity of the studied organizations. Both young organizations and startups (Kannothra et al., 2018; Siebold et al., 2019; Yin & Chen, 2019) and large enterprises (Gibbons & Hazy, 2017;

Sarhangi et al., 2021) have growth aspirations. However, these growth aspirations are a significant source of challenges for SEs due to their hybrid nature (Kannothra et al., 2018).

The literature shows how organizations have successfully navigated this process and increased their relative hybridity. For example, these organizations have undergone a transformation to become SEs (Liu & Ko, 2012). Maibom and Smith (2016) studied a nonprofit organization for which the market logic became more important over time. A change in legal form can facilitate such a transformation (Siwale et al., 2021). Furthermore, Kurland and Schneper (2021) investigated how a profit-oriented company became an SE. Over time, it incorporated a social mission and developed with four different legal forms over a 45 year span. In addition, Sarma (2020) investigated two microfinance organizations in India, as they have retained their social goals in the commercialization process.

SEs address complex social problems. A clear vision and a shared organizational goal are of significant importance and can help increase focus and reduce complexity (Crucke et al., 2015; Kokko, 2018). The vision should be established so that it covers a long time frame. A willingness to significantly change organizational structure and legal forms might be necessary to remain within the guidelines of the vision. External influences, such as the financial crisis in 2008, can further complicate the process (Ramus et al., 2016). The organizational culture in SEs should be particularly flexible to address challenges arising from complex institutional demands (Voltan & De Fuentes, 2016). Scholars propose enabling an interplay between collaboration and formalization, or a structured form of flexibility (Ramus et al., 2016; Smith & Besharov, 2019).

To make these challenges more manageable, scholars have provided focused guiding principles for increasing the degree of hybridity. By concentrating on specific areas, the management of hybridity can be compartmentalized into distinct organizational departments. For example, Hsieh et al. (2018) took a values-centered approach and proposed that positive outcomes can be achieved by focusing on three stages in human resource management: attracting, selecting and socializing employees. Furthermore, the provision of products and services can be guided by involved searching, dialogic localizing and engaged implementing (Sengupta et al., 2020). Kurland and Schneper (2021) listed the central phases of a firm's hybridization process as animating, cultivating, advocating and sustaining. Furthermore, Dufays (2019) focused on different stages of innovation management. Marketing (Liu & Ko, 2012) and legitimacy building (Yang & Wu, 2016) have also been investigated.

Discussion

This study details a comprehensive framework for the management of hybridity in SEs. First, the positioning of relative hybridity should occur. SEs can either prioritize the social or economic logic or consider these logics to be equally important. This positioning is not necessarily the same at the individual and organizational levels, nor should it remain constant over time. The oscillation of relative hybridity should be facilitated. Diverse integration and differentiation strategies act as bridging mechanisms to facilitate the achievement of a shared goal. Second, guardrails should be erected as thresholds or early warning systems. Guardrails can be set up for a single logic or for both logics. Individual and organizational guardrails should be regarded separately. Furthermore, a focus on internal and external guardrails is essential. While the social or economic mission can internally be guarded by strong leadership or certain metrics, external guardrails that are provided through stakeholder relationships can serve to avoid low levels of relative hybridity. Guardrails are especially important because they can reduce institutional complexity for organizational members. Third, a long-term perspective should not be neglected in the aim of successfully increasing the degree of hybridity in SEs. Because SEs address complex social problems, they should be guided by a shared vision. Particularly as a SE grows, targeted strategies for organizational areas become important.

This framework has been developed from a comprehensive understanding of the literature so that findings from one paper might find application in all three areas of the framework. In addition to the framework, the process also revealed scholarly research orientations. The 82 identified articles can be grouped into three categories: (1) social entrepreneurs and their skills, (2) a specific organizational area of management and (3) overarching guiding principles. This further provides insights for scholars into their own approach when studying the management of hybridity in the SE context.

This paper contributes to the SE literature by identifying concrete and actionable mechanisms for managing hybridity. Early scholarly work in the field of social entrepreneurship has been focused around outlining definitional aspects. This study advances the field by identifying managerial practices that are particular to SEs (Dacin et al., 2010) by investigating strategies for managing different degrees of hybridity. Furthermore, there are theoretical implications for organizational hybridity and social entrepreneurship research. A widely discussed dichotomy inherent to the nature of hybridity divides scholars into those who view them as synergetic (Battilana & Dorado, 2010) and those who view them as detrimental to each other (Austin et al., 2006; Siwale et al., 2021; Woodside, 2018). From the perspective of a detrimental relationship, social and economic goals are viewed as a zero-sum game (Teasdale, 2012). Hence, a decrease in social value is required to maximize commercial value. Conversely, the perspective of a synergetic relationship identifies mission spill-over effects that signify an overall benefit of the hybrid approach (Hockerts, 2015; Kurland & Schneper, 2021; Munoz & Kimmitt, 2019; Siebold et al., 2019). The approach of identifying the correct perspective is prevalent in the literature on paradox theory (Lewis, 2000; Lüscher & Lewis, 2008; Miron-Spektor et al., 2018) or in previous reviews (Smith et al., 2013). In contrast, in the present study, both outcomes are possible, as the outcome depends on the effectiveness of managerial practices.

Furthermore, this study has practical implications. The aggregation of managerial strategies based on the framework by Shepherd et al. (2019) is particularly helpful for practitioners in SEs in offering guidance in the management of hybridity. A holistic governance approach to the management of hybridity should cover positioning, guardrail setting and increasing the degree of hybridity. This framework is not only relevant for SEs. Businesses aiming to integrate a social mission and nonprofit organizations aiming to integrate an economic mission in their activities can also apply the framework. Both of these scenarios are becoming increasingly prevalent in practice (Hersberger-Langloh et al., 2021; Porter & Kramer, 2011).

Conclusion: Limitations and Future Research

Due to the increase in studies on hybridity management in SEs, this literature review provides a significant theoretical and practical contribution to the portrayal of recent findings. The identification of research orientations provides an overview of the scholarly approaches to the study of hybridity management. The investigation of the relationship between social and economic missions in SEs is timely (Fu, 2023). However, this study has certain limitations. It is limited by its sole focus on the duality of social and economic logics. This binary and exclusive relationship between social and economic missions has been called into question (Munoz & Kimmitt, 2019). In practice, SEs are often influenced by more than two institutional logics (Siegner et al., 2018). There are specific institutional logics that significantly influence SEs' activities according to their industry. The author agrees that additional research on the relationship between more than two logics is needed (Battilana et al., 2017). Further limitations relate to the literature review process. Despite the application of backward snowballing, the omission of forward snowballing may have resulted in the exclusion of relevant articles. Additionally, this study focused on publications in peer-reviewed journals and excluded gray literature. The negligible number of results for articles published before 2012 indicates that the topic is rather new. However, the concept of managing hybridity has been investigated prior to that date but simply termed differently. The concept has also been investigated in other organizations prior to research on SEs becoming prevalent. Hence, similar relevant studies may have potentially been excluded. In addition, related research is still focused on the global north. Although four case studies have been conducted, for example, in Africa and South America, the majority of related research has taken place in Europe. Hence, other contexts are still represented to a limited degree. More research into the differences across institutional contexts between regions or countries could provide further insight into the management of hybridity in SEs (Mair & Rathert, 2020). In particular, the influence of government is large in the development of SE ecosystems. Thus, this topic should be investigated further. In particular, insights into hybridity management over longer time periods could reveal new insights. However, longitudinal research over long time spans is still rare. Further, additional quantitative research is needed to test the hypotheses gained from explorative qualitative studies. To date, only six studies in the sample have employed quantitative methods, and only five have used mixed methods. This approach is particularly timely, as validated measurement scales now enable the conceptualization of different degrees of hybridity (Fu, 2023; Lortie et al., 2024; Stevens et al., 2015). Finally, a large part of the literature on managing hybridity has focused on SEs (Ratinho & Bruneel, 2024). The management of two logics is becoming more important for other organizations and should be investigated in a variety of institutional contexts.

References

Alberti, F. G., & Varon Garrido, M. A. (2017). Can profit and sustainability goals co-exist? New business models for hybrid firms. *Journal of Business Strategy, 38*(1), 3-13.

Alsaid, L., & Ambilichu, C. A. (2021). The influence of institutional pressures on the implementation of a performance measurement system in an Egyptian social enterprise. *Qualitative Research in Accounting and Management, 18*(1), 53-83.

André, K., & Pache, A.-C. (2016). From Caring Entrepreneur to Caring Enterprise: Addressing the Ethical Challenges of Scaling up Social Enterprises. *Journal of Business Ethics, 133*(4), 659-675.

Ashforth, B. E., & Reingen, P. H. (2014). Functions of Dysfunction: Managing the Dynamics of an Organizational Duality in a Natural Food Cooperative. *Administrative Science Quarterly, 59*(3), 474-516.

Åstebro, T., & Hoos, F. (2021). Impact measurement based on repeated randomized control trials: The case of a training program to encourage social entrepreneurship. *Strategic Entrepreneurship Journal, 15*, 254-278.

Austin, J., Stevenson, H., & Wei–Skillern, J. (2006). Social and Commercial Entrepreneurship: Same, Different, or Both? *Entrepreneurship Theory and Practice, 30*(1), 1-22.

Bacq, S., Hartog, C., & Hoogendoorn, B. (2013). A Quantitative Comparison of Social and Commercial Entrepreneurship: Toward a More Nuanced Understanding of Social Entrepreneurship Organizations in Context. *Journal of Social Entrepreneurship, 4*(1), 40-68.

Battilana, J. (2018). Cracking the organizational challenge of pursuing joint social and financial goals: Social enterprise as a laboratory to understand hybrid organizing. *M@n@gement, 21*(4), 1278-1305.

Battilana, J., Besharov, M. L., & Mitzinneck, B. C. (2017). On hybrids and hybrid organizing: A review and roadmap for future research.

Battilana, J., & Dorado, S. (2010). Building Sustainable Hybrid Organizations: The Case of Commercial Microfinance Organizations. *The Academy of Management Journal, 53*(6), 1419-1440.

Battilana, J., & Lee, M. (2014). Advancing Research on Hybrid Organizing - Insights from the Study of Social Enterprises. *Academy of Management Annals, 8*(1), 397-441.

Battilana, J., Sengul, M., Pache, A.-C., & Model, J. (2015). Harnessing Productive Tensions in Hybrid Organizations: The Case of Work Integration Social Enterprises. *Academy of Management Journal, 58*(6), 1658-1685.

Bengtsson, M. (2016). How to plan and perform a qualitative study using content analysis. *NursingPlus Open, 2*, 8-14.

Besharov, M. L., & Smith, W. K. (2014). Multiple Institutional Logics in Organizations: Explaining Their Varied Nature and Implications. *Academy of Management Review, 39*(3), 364-381.

Billis, D. (2010). Towards a theory of hybrid organizations. In D. Billis (Ed.), *Hybrid organizations and the third sector: Challenges for practice, theory and policy* (pp. 46-69). Basingstoke, Hampshire, UK: Palgrave Macmillan.

Bonomi, S., Ricciardi, F., Rossignoli, C., & Zardini, A. (2021). Cocreating resilient hybrids: the bridging power of social enterprises' organizational logics. *International Journal of Entrepreneurial Behavior & Research, 27*(2), 470-495.

Bruneel, J., Clarysse, B., Weemaes, S., & Staessens, M. (2020). Breaking With the Past: The Need for Innovation in the Governance of Nonprofit Social Enterprises. *Academy of Management Perspectives, 34*(2), 209-225.

Canclini, N. G. (2015). Hybridity. In J. D. Wright (Ed.), *International Encyclopedia of the Social & Behavioral Sciences (Second Edition)* (pp. 448-452). Oxford: Elsevier.

Castellas, E. I., Stubbs, W., & Ambrosini, V. (2019). Responding to Value Pluralism in Hybrid Organizations. *Journal of Business Ethics, 159*(3), 635-650.

Chell, E. (2007). Social Enterprise and Entrepreneurship: Towards a Convergent Theory of the Entrepreneurial Process. *International Small Business Journal, 25*(1), 5-26.

Child, C. (2020). Whence Paradox? Framing Away the Potential Challenges of Doing Well by Doing Good in Social Enterprise Organizations. *Organization Studies, 41*(8), 1147-1167, Article 0170840619857467.

Ciambotti, G., & Pedrini, M. (2021). Hybrid Harvesting Strategies to Overcome Resource Constraints: Evidence from Social Enterprises in Kenya. *Journal of Business Ethics, 168*(3), 631-650.

Cornelissen, J. P., Akemu, O., Jonkman, J. G. F., & Werner, M. D. (2021). Building Character: The Formation of a Hybrid Organizational Identity in a Social Enterprise. *Journal of Management Studies, 58*(5), 1294-1330.

Cornforth, C. (2014). Understanding and combating mission drift in social enterprises. *Social Enterprise Journal, 10*(1), 3-20.

Costanzo, L. A., Vurro, C., Foster, D., Servato, F., & Perrini, F. (2014). Dual-Mission Management in Social Entrepreneurship: Qualitative Evidence from Social Firms in the United Kingdom. *Journal of Small Business Management, 52*(4), 655-677.

Crucke, S., Moray, N., & Vallet, N. (2015). Internal Representation and Factional Faultlines as Antecedents for Board Performance in Social Enterprises. *Annals of Public and Cooperative Economics, 86*(2), 385-400.

Dacin, P. A., Dacin, M. T., & Matear, M. (2010). Social Entrepreneurship: Why We Don't Need a New Theory and How We Move Forward From Here. *Academy of Management Perspectives, 24*(3), 37-57.

Davies, I. A., & Doherty, B. (2019). Balancing a Hybrid Business Model: The Search for Equilibrium at Cafedirect. *Journal of Business Ethics, 157*(4), 1043-1066.

Davies, I. A., Haugh, H., & Chambers, L. (2019). Barriers to Social Enterprise Growth. *Journal of Small Business Management, 57*(4), 1616-1636.

Dees, J. G. (1998). Enterprising nonprofits. *Harvard Business Review, 76*(1), 55-67.

Di Maggio, P. J., & Powell, W. W. (1983). The Iron Cage Revisited: Institutional Isomorphism and Collective Rationality in Organizational Fields. *American Sociological Review, 48*(2), 147-160.

Dufays, F. (2019). Exploring the drivers of tensions in social innovation management in the context of social entrepreneurial teams. *Management Decision, 57*(6), 1344-1361.

Dunn, M. B., & Jones, C. (2010). Institutional Logics and Institutional Pluralism: The Contestation of Care and Science Logics in Medical Education, 1967–2005. *Administrative Science Quarterly, 55*(1), 114-149.

Ebrahim, A., Battilana, J., & Mair, J. (2014). The governance of social enterprises: Mission drift and accountability challenges in hybrid organizations. *Research in Organizational Behavior, 34*, 81-100.

European Commission. (2021). *Social Economy Action Plan*. Retrieved 27 February 2024 from https://ec.europa.eu/social/main.jsp?catId=1537&langId=en

Evers, A. (2005). Mixed Welfare Systems and Hybrid Organizations: Changes in the Governance and Provision of Social Services. *International Journal of Public Administration, 28*(9-10), 737-748.

Fu, J. S. (2023). Social-Market Hybridity in Social Ventures: Scale Development and Validation. *Business & Society, 0*(0), 00076503231167569.

Gehringer, T. (2021). Corporate Foundations as Hybrid Organizations: A Systematic Review of Literature. *VOLUNTAS: International Journal of Voluntary and Nonprofit Organizations, 32*(2), 257-275.

Gibbons, J., & Hazy, J. K. (2017). Leading a Large-Scale Distributed Social Enterprise: How the Leadership Culture at Goodwill Industries Creates and Distributes Value in Communities. *Nonprofit Management & Leadership*, *27*(3), 299-316.

Grimes, M. G., Williams, T. A., & Zhao, E. Y. (2019). Anchors Aweigh: The Sources, Variety, and Challenges of Mission Drift. *Academy of Management Review*, *44*(4), 819-845.

Hahn, T. (2020). Business Sustainability as a Context for Studying Hybridity. In M. L. Besharov & B. C. Mitzinneck (Eds.), *Organizational Hybridity: Perspectives, Processes, Promises* (Vol. 69, pp. 115-138). Emerald Publishing Limited.

Haigh, N., & Hoffman, A. (2012). Hybrid Organizations: The Next Chapter of Sustainable Business. *Organizational Dynamics*, *41*, 126–134.

Haigh, N., & Hoffman, A. J. (2014). The New Heretics: Hybrid Organizations and the Challenges They Present to Corporate Sustainability. *Organization & Environment*, *27*(3), 223-241.

Hersberger-Langloh, S. E., Stühlinger, S., & von Schnurbein, G. (2021). Institutional isomorphism and nonprofit managerialism: For better or worse? *Nonprofit Management and Leadership*, *31*(3), 461-480.

Hockerts, K. (2015). How Hybrid Organizations Turn Antagonistic Assets into Complementarities. *California Management Review*, *57*(3), 83-106.

Hoffman, A., Badiane, K., & Haigh, N. (2012). Hybrid Organizations as Agents of Positive Social Change: Bridging the For-profit & Non-profit Divide. In *Using a Positive Lens to Explore Social Change and Organizations*. Routledge.

Hsieh, Y. C., Weng, J. J., & Lin, T. (2018). How social enterprises manage their organizational identification: a theoretical framework of identity management approach through attraction, selection, and socialization. *International Journal of Human Resource Management*, *29*(20), 2880-2904.

Imperatori, B., & Ruta, D. C. (2015). Designing a social enterprise Organization configuration and social stakeholders' work involvement. *Social Enterprise Journal*, *11*(3), 321-+.

Ismail, A., & Johnson, B. (2019). Managing Organizational Paradoxes in Social Enterprises: Case Studies from the MENA Region [Article]. *Voluntas*, *30*(3), 516-534.

Jin, B. (2020). The Practical Intelligence of Social Entrepreneurs: Managing the Hybridity of Social Enterprises. *Entrepreneurship Research Journal*, *10*(1), 19, Article 20180007.

Kannampuzha, M., & Hockerts, K. (2019). Organizational social entrepreneurship: scale development and validation. *Social Enterprise Journal*, *15*(3), 290-319.

Kannothra, C. G., Manning, S., & Haigh, N. (2018). How Hybrids Manage Growth and Social-Business Tensions in Global Supply Chains: The Case of Impact Sourcing. *Journal of Business Ethics*, *148*(2), 271-290.

Kibler, E., Wincent, J., Kautonen, T., Cacciotti, G., & Obschonka, M. (2019). Can prosocial motivation harm entrepreneurs' subjective well-being? *Journal of Business Venturing*, *34*(4), 608-624.

Kim, D., Cho, W., & Allen, B. (2020). Sustainability of social economy organizations (SEOs): An analysis of the conditions for surviving and thriving. *The Social Science Journal*, 1-17.

Kokko, S. (2018). Social entrepreneurship: creating social value when bridging holes. *Social Enterprise Journal*, *14*(4), 410-428.

Krippendorff, K. (2004). *Content Analysis: An Introduction to Its Methodology* (2nd ed.). Thousand Oaks, CA: Sage Publications.

Kurland, N. B., & Schneper, W. D. (2021). A Social Enterprise's Hybridising Journey to Reconcile Goals and Structure with Identity. *Journal of Social Entrepreneurship*, 1-26.

Lewis, M. W. (2000). Exploring Paradox: Toward a More Comprehensive Guide. *The Academy of Management Review*, *25*(4), 760-776.

Liu, G., & Ko, W. W. (2012). Organizational Learning and Marketing Capability Development: A Study of the Charity Retailing Operations of British Social Enterprise. *Nonprofit and Voluntary Sector Quarterly*, *41*(4), 580-608.

Lortie, J., Cox, K. C., Castro, S., & Castrogiovanni, G. J. (2024). Measuring Social Entrepreneurship: Identifying and Assessing the Performance of Social Entrepreneurial Ventures. *Journal of Social Entrepreneurship*, 1-29.

Lumpkin, G. T., Moss, T. W., Gras, D. M., Kato, S., & Amezcua, A. S. (2013). Entrepreneurial processes in social contexts: how are they different, if at all? *Small Business Economics*, *40*(3), 761-783.

Lüscher, L. S., & Lewis, M. W. (2008). Organizational Change and Managerial Sensemaking: Working Through Paradox. *Academy of Management Journal*, *51*(2), 221-240.

Maibom, C., & Smith, P. (2016). Symbiosis across institutional logics in a social enterprise. *Social Enterprise Journal*, *12*(3), 260-280.

Maier, F., Meyer, M., & Steinbereithner, M. (2014). Nonprofit Organizations Becoming Business-Like: A Systematic Review. *Nonprofit and Voluntary Sector Quarterly*, *45*(1), 64-86.

Mair, J., & Martí, I. (2006). Social entrepreneurship research: A source of explanation, prediction, and delight. *Journal of World Business*, *41*(1), 36-44.

Mair, J., Mayer, J., & Lutz, E. (2015). Navigating Institutional Plurality: Organizational Governance in Hybrid Organizations. *Organization Studies*, *36*(6), 713-739.

Mair, J., & Rathert, N. (2020). Let's Talk about Problems: Advancing Research on Hybrid Organizing, Social Enterprises, and Institutional Context. In M. L. Besharov & B. C. Mitzinneck (Eds.), *Organizational Hybridity: Perspectives, Processes, Promises* (Vol. 69, pp. 189-208). Emerald Publishing Limited.

Mallett, R., Hagen-Zanker, J., Slater, R., & Duvendack, M. (2012). The benefits and challenges of using systematic reviews in international development research. *Journal of Development Effectiveness*, *4*(3), 445-455.

Mason, C., & Doherty, B. (2016). A Fair Trade-off? Paradoxes in the Governance of Fair-trade Social Enterprises. *Journal of Business Ethics*, *136*(3), 451-469.

Matzembacher, D. E., Raudsaar, M., de Barcellos, M. D., & Mets, T. (2020). Business Models' Innovations to Overcome Hybridity-Related Tensions in Sustainable Entrepreneurship. *Sustainability*, *12*(11), 17, Article 4503.

McMullen, J. S. (2018). Organizational hybrids as biological hybrids: Insights for research on the relationship between social enterprise and the entrepreneurial ecosystem. *Journal of Business Venturing*, *33*(5), 575-590.

Miron-Spektor, E., Ingram, A., Keller, J., Smith, W. K., & Lewis, M. W. (2018). Microfoundations of Organizational Paradox: The Problem Is How We Think about the Problem. *Academy of Management Journal*, *61*(1), 26-45.

Mitzinneck, B. C., & Besharov, M. L. (2019). Managing Value Tensions in Collective Social Entrepreneurship: The Role of Temporal, Structural, and Collaborative Compromise. *Journal of Business Ethics*, *159*(2), 381-400.

Mongelli, L., Rullani, F., Ramus, T., & Rimac, T. (2019). The Bright Side of Hybridity: Exploring How Social Enterprises Manage and Leverage Their Hybrid Nature. *Journal of Business Ethics*, *159*(2), 301-305.

Morris, M. H., Santos, S. C., & Kuratko, D. F. (2020). The great divides in social entrepreneurship and where they lead us. *Small Business Economics*, *57*, 1089–1106.

Munoz, P., & Kimmitt, J. (2019). Social mission as competitive advantage: A configurational analysis of the strategic conditions of social entrepreneurship. *Journal of Business Research*, *101*, 854-861.

Ometto, M. P., Gegenhuber, T., Winter, J., & Greenwood, R. (2019). From Balancing Missions to Mission Drift: The Role of the Institutional Context, Spaces, and

Compartmentalization in the Scaling of Social Enterprises. *Business & Society, 58*(5), 1003-1046.

Pache, A.-C., & Santos, F. (2013a). Embedded in Hybrid Contexts: How Individuals in Organizations Respond to Competing Institutional Logics. In M. Lounsbury & E. Boxenbaum (Eds.), *Institutional Logics in Action, Part B* (Vol. 39 Part B, pp. 3-35). Emerald Group Publishing Limited.

Pache, A.-C., & Santos, F. (2013b). Inside the Hybrid Organization: Selective Coupling as a Response to Competing Institutional Logics. *Academy of Management Journal, 56*(4), 972-1001.

Park, J. H. (2020). Chasing two rabbits: how social enterprises as hybrid organizations manage paradoxes. *Asian Business & Management, 19*(4), 407-437.

Pellegrini, G., Annosi, M. C., Conto, F., & Fiore, M. (2020). What Are the Conflicting Tensions in an Italian Cooperative and How Do Members Manage Them? Business Goals', Integrated Management, and Reduction of Waste within a Fruit and Vegetables Supply Chain. *Sustainability, 12*(7), 15, Article 3050.

Perrini, F., Vurro, C., & Costanzo, L. A. (2010). A process-based view of social entrepreneurship: From opportunity identification to scaling-up social change in the case of San Patrignano. *Entrepreneurship & Regional Development, 22*(6), 515-534.

Petticrew, M., & Roberts, H. (2006). *Systematic Reviews in the Social Sciences: A Practical Guide.* Malden, MA.: Blackwell Publishing Ltd.

Porter, M., & Kramer, M. (2011). The Big Idea: Creating Shared Value. How to Reinvent Capitalism—and Unleash a Wave of Innovation and Growth. *Harvard Business Review, 89*, 62-77.

Powell, M., Gillett, A., & Doherty, B. (2019). Sustainability in social enterprise: hybrid organizing in public services. *Public Management Review, 21*(2), 159-186.

Powell, W. W., & Sandholtz, K. W. (2012). Amphibious entrepreneurs and the emergence of organizational forms. *Strategic Entrepreneurship Journal, 6*(2), 94-115.

Ramus, T., & Vaccaro, A. (2017). Stakeholders Matter: How Social Enterprises Address Mission Drift. *Journal of Business Ethics, 143*(2), 307-322.

Ramus, T., Vaccaro, A., & Brusoni, S. (2016). Institutional Complexity in Turbulent Times: Formalization, Collaboration, and the Emergence of Blended Logics. *Academy of Management Journal, 60*(4), 1253-1284.

Ratinho, T., & Bruneel, J. (2024). Taking stock of research on hybrid organizations: Enriching theoretical perspectives, extending empirical contexts, and expanding practical relevance. *Journal of Business Research, 170*, 114313.

Reuter, E. (2022). Hybrid business models in the sharing economy: The role of business model design for managing the environmental paradox. *Business Strategy and the Environment, 31*(2), 603-618.

Sadiq, T., Tulder, R. v., & Maas, K. (2022). Building a Taxonomy of Hybridization: An Institutional Logics Perspective on Societal Impact. *Sustainability, 14*(16), 10301.

Sanzo-Pérez, M. J., Rey-García, M., & Álvarez-González, L. I. (2021). Downward accountability to beneficiaries in social enterprises: do partnerships with nonprofits boost it without undermining accountability to other stakeholders? *Review of Managerial Science.*

Sarhangi, R., Mashayekhi, A. N., & Souzanchi Kashani, E. (2021). From Black and White to Yin and Yang: Exploring the Management of Tensions in Social Enterprises. *Journal of Social Entrepreneurship*, 1-25.

Sarma, S. K. (2020). Retaining the social goal: role of path creation in for-profit social enterprises. *Journal of Management History, 26*(1), 77-98.

Schröer, A., & Jäger, U. (2015). Beyond Balancing?: A Research Agenda on Leadership in Hybrid Organizations. *International Studies of Management & Organization*, *45*(3), 259-281.

Seibel, W. (2015). Studying Hybrids: Sectors and Mechanisms. *Organization Studies*, *36*(6), 697-712.

Sengupta, S., Sahay, A., & Hisrich, R. D. (2020). The social - market convergence in a renewable energy social enterprise. *Journal of Cleaner Production*, *270*, 15, Article 122516.

Shepherd, D. A., Williams, T. A., & Zhao, E. Y. (2019). A Framework for Exploring the Degree of Hybridity in Entrepreneurship. *Academy of Management Perspectives*, *33*(4), 491-512.

Siebold, N., Gunzel-Jensen, F., & Muller, S. (2019). Balancing dual missions for social venture growth: a comparative case study. *Entrepreneurship and Regional Development*, *31*(9-10), 710-734.

Siegner, M., Pinkse, J., & Panwar, R. (2018). Managing tensions in a social enterprise: The complex balancing act to deliver a multi-faceted but coherent social mission. *Journal of Cleaner Production*, *174*, 1314-1324.

Simatele, M., & Dlamini, P. (2020). Finance and the social mission: a quest for sustainability and inclusion. *Qualitative Research in Financial Markets*, *12*(2), 225-242.

Siwale, J., Kimmitt, J., & Amankwah-Amoah, J. (2021). The Failure of Hybrid Organizations: A Legitimation Perspective. *Management and Organization Review*, *17*(3), 452-485.

Skelcher, C., & Smith, S. R. (2015). Theorizing Hybridity: Institutional Logics, Complex Organizations, and Actor Identities: The Case of Nonprofits. *Public Administration*, *93*(2), 433-448.

Smith, S. R. (2014). Hybridity and Nonprofit Organizations: The Research Agenda. *American Behavioral Scientist*, *58*(11), 1494-1508.

Smith, W. K., & Besharov, M. L. (2019). Bowing before Dual Gods: How Structured Flexibility Sustains Organizational Hybridity. *Administrative Science Quarterly*, *64*(1), 1-44.

Smith, W. K., Besharov, M. L., Wessels, A. K., & Chertok, M. (2012). A Paradoxical Leadership Model for Social Entrepreneurs: Challenges, Leadership Skills, and Pedagogical Tools for Managing Social and Commercial Demands. *Academy of Management Learning & Education*, *11*(3), 463-478.

Smith, W. K., Gonin, M., & Besharov, M. L. (2013). Managing Social-Business Tensions: A Review and Research Agenda for Social Enterprise. *Business Ethics Quarterly*, *23*(3), 407-442.

Stevens, R., Moray, N., & Bruneel, J. (2015). The Social and Economic Mission of Social Enterprises: Dimensions, Measurement, Validation, and Relation. *Entrepreneurship Theory and Practice*, *39*(5), 1051-1082.

Teasdale, S. (2012). Negotiating Tensions: How Do Social Enterprises in the Homelessness Field Balance Social and Commercial Considerations? *Housing Studies*, *27*(4), 514-532.

Timulak, L. (2007). Identifying core categories of client-identified impact of helpful events in psychotherapy: A qualitative meta-analysis. *Psychotherapy Research*, *17*(3), 305-314.

Timulak, L. (2009). Meta-analysis of qualitative studies: A tool for reviewing qualitative research findings in psychotherapy. *Psychotherapy Research*, *19*(4-5), 591-600.

Timulak, L. (2014). Qualitative Meta-Analysis. In *The SAGE Handbook of Qualitative Data Analysis* (pp. 481-495). SAGE Publications Ltd

Tranfield, D., Denyer, D., & Smart, P. (2003). Towards a Methodology for Developing Evidence-Informed Management Knowledge by Means of Systematic Review. *British Journal of Management*, *14*(3), 207-222.

Tykkylainen, S., & Ritala, P. (2021). Business model innovation in social enterprises: An activity system perspective. *Journal of Business Research*, *125*, 684-697.

Voltan, A., & De Fuentes, C. (2016). Managing multiple logics in partnerships for scaling social innovation. *European Journal of Innovation Management*, *19*(4), 446-467.

Wagenschwanz, A. M., & Grimes, M. G. (2021). Navigating compromise: How founder authenticity affects venture identification amidst organizational hybridity. *Journal of Business Venturing*, *36*(2), 18, Article 106085.

Weerawardena, J., & Mort, G. S. (2006). Investigating social entrepreneurship: A multidimensional model. *Journal of World Business*, *41*(1), 21-35.

Westley, F. R., & McConnell, J. (2010). Making a Difference: Strategies for Scaling Social Innovation for Greater Impact. *The Innovation Journal: The Public Sector Innovation Journal*, *15*(2).

Williamson, O. E. (1985). *The Economic Institutions of Capitalism: Firms, Markets, Relational Contracting*. New York: The Free Press.

Wohlin, C. (2014). *Guidelines for snowballing in systematic literature studies and a replication in software engineering* Proceedings of the 18th International Conference on Evaluation and Assessment in Software Engineering, London, United Kingdom. https://doi.org/10.1145/2601248.2601268

Woodside, S. J. (2018). Dominant logics US WISEs and the tendency to favor a market-dominant or social mission-dominant approach. *Social Enterprise Journal*, *14*(1), 39-59.

Yang, Y. K., & Wu, S. L. (2016). In search of the right fusion recipe: the role of legitimacy in building a social enterprise model. *Business Ethics-a European Review*, *25*(3), 327-343.

Yin, J. L., & Chen, H. (2019). Dual-goal management in social enterprises: evidence from China. *Management Decision*, *57*(6), 1362-1381.

Zur, A. (2020). Entrepreneurial Identity and Social-Business Tensions - The Experience of Social Entrepreneurs. *Journal of Social Entrepreneurship*, 24.

Essay Two

From Social Worker to Social Entrepreneur: Dynamic Proximity in a Social Impact Incubator

Lucca Nietlispach

Abstract

Social impact incubators (SIIs) provide structured programs for social entrepreneurs to support them in their endeavors to solve wicked problems. The resources provided by these programs are intended to enable social entrepreneurs to contribute to systems change through establishing economically sustainable organizations. However, there is a limited understanding of how interaction, learning, and organizational development occur within SII programs. The aim of this study was to identify specific mechanisms through a holistic single case study in the empirical setting of an SII program in Germany. Data was collected through semi-structured interviews, ethnographic participation, and documentation over the span of 10 months. Structuration theory and different dimensions of proximity guided the analysis. The theories also informed the model of dynamic proximity that was developed. The findings indicate that there were two opposing interaction mechanisms of the SII-program participants: proximity moderation and proximity augmentation. Participants augmented their proximity in relation to cognitive, social, institutional, and spatial dimensions. Their knowledge of and identification with social entrepreneurship increased significantly during the program. However, proximity was also moderated in other instances, and lock-in was purposefully avoided. By identifying changes and mechanisms of dynamic proximity in an empirical setting, this research contributes to the literature on proximity.

Keywords: social entrepreneurship, social innovation, social impact incubator, social incubator, proximity

Introduction

Many social issues have been described as wicked problems due to their persistent nature and the complexity involved in solving them (Dorado & Ventresca, 2013; Santos, 2012; Waddock et al., 2015). One potential solution to such problems is combining the management of social and economic goals, but this form of "hybrid organizing" is characterized by tensions (Greenwood et al., 2011). Many founders aim to build hybrid organizations that combine social and economic goals. Although they are usually driven by the desire to address a wicked problem, they lack the necessary knowledge and resources to do so. In their effort to close this gap, social impact incubators (SIIs) offer programs to support founders in their entrepreneurial endeavors. Casasnovas and Bruno (2013) defined SIIs as "programs that support the scaling process of organizations that mainly target social challenges through innovative and market-oriented solutions" (p. 180). Their support activities can take different forms and range from prices and awards to funding and managerial support. By imparting business-related skills as well as knowledge about impact measurement and the larger ecosystem, SIIs expose entrepreneurs to two guiding logics of social and economic value creation (Roundy, 2017). However, questions have arisen about educating social entrepreneurs on hybrid organizing (Fahrenwald et al., 2021; Pache & Chowdhury, 2012; Thomsen et al., 2021; Tracey & Phillips, 2007). For one, the sets of skills that social entrepreneurs apply are different from the business context (Cajaiba-Santana, 2014). In addition, the importance of the social mission and the scarcity of resources pose different challenges for SIIs in developing a program curriculum and their specific services.

Despite these concerns, the number of incubators focusing on nonprofit organizations and social enterprises is increasing. Their activities are also highly relevant for policymakers, as promoting the education of social entrepreneurs is one of the areas of the Social Economy Action Plan published by the European Commission (2021). Considering that these incubators have rarely been studied and that there is a limited understanding of their activities, this research aims to investigate the interactions of the participants in an SII program. This will provide a better understanding of their learning process and will allow new programs to be implemented more efficiently, thereby hopefully improving the capacity of founders to address wicked problems. The research question is the following:

How do interactions and the learning process take place in SII programs?

An SII program conducted by Grünhof will serve as a case study. Grünhof is an organization with several locations in Freiburg, southern Germany. They conduct multiple incubation and acceleration programs. The program analyzed in this study focuses on nascent ventures with a strong social aim and the potential to build an economically sustainable organization. It is conducted by the Social Innovation Lab, which is an organizational unit of Grünhof.

Following research about the importance of spatiality, this study will describe the local ecosystem in which the SII is situated (Grohs et al., 2017). In the field of social innovation, local and regional development has become an important research topic (Domanski et al., 2019; von Schnurbein et al., 2021). However, not only the spatial dimension but also the cognitive, social, and institutional dimensions of proximity serve as conceptual lenses for investigating the research question (Boschma, 2005).

The next chapter elucidates the theoretical background. Before turning to the different dimensions of proximity and their relevance, it situates the dynamic nature of SII programs within structuration theory (Giddens, 1986). Structuration theory provides a foundation for understanding the relationship between structures and agents generally. Following the chapter on the theoretical background, the research design, data collection, and analysis are described in a chapter on methodology. Then the findings regarding how the participants interacted and learned in the SII program are presented. Finally, the findings and implications for future research are discussed.

Theoretical Background

Structuration Theory in Social Entrepreneurship

The most significant contribution of Giddens's (1986) theory of structuration is its combination of structure and agency. This "duality of structure" alludes to how structures are concurrently the result and medium of social action. Structures and agency are thus mutually constitutive. This means that structures have a significant effect on how agents behave, but the behavior of agents also changes the structures. In the context of social entrepreneurship, structuration theory suggests that the entrepreneur and social systems evolve together. Structuration theory is general and broad in its application. The possibility of application in a specific context warrants a detailed investigation of the concepts to be applied in the analysis. Due to its interest in how SII-program participants learn, this study focused more on how the structure of the incubation program influenced the agents, rather than how the agents influenced the structure. Despite this focus on the institutional realm and not on the action realm (Jarzabkowski, 2008), it remained important for the analysis to take into consideration the theory in its entirety.

Structure is understood to be the principles that pattern social practices (Sewell, 1992). It consists of schemas and resources. Schemas, also called knowledge structures, are templates imposed on a situation in order to interpret it (Walsh, 1995). Particularly in novel situations, they help interpret stimuli (Labianca et al., 2000). They imply an essentially theory-driven view of how individuals approach new knowledge. Schemas are comparable to rules but place equal weight on enabling social practices rather than just on constraining them. Schemas can exist on the individual and group level. The larger the congruence between a schema on both levels, the more an individual is part of a specific collective (Merali, 2000). Examples of schemas include rules of etiquette, aesthetic norms, and recipes for group action (Sewell, 1992). In the context of social entrepreneurship, schemas are strongly influenced by hybridity. For example, social entrepreneurs value inclusion and a collaborative approach above wealth maximization. Finally, schemas are dynamic and can change over time (Bartunek, 1984). They are virtual in nature because they are generalizable and transposable to new situations. Conversely, resources are not virtual but real. Resources are the media through which transformative capacity is realized (Giddens, 1986). They can be differentiated between human and nonhuman resources. The control of resources allows the maintenance of power (Sewell, 1992).

The definition of agency in its simplest form is simply what individuals do (Giddens, 1986). Both habitual and purposive actions are part of the action realm. Agents are purposive in the sense that they are knowledgeable and able to reflect on their interpretation of social systems (Sarason et al., 2006). Agents are engaged in the reproduction of structures, which takes place as a response to problems that arise in historical situations. Due to the different backgrounds of the structural environments of social entrepreneurs, their interpretations of social systems can differ. That is why they may act as agents in different ways in the pursuit of opportunities.

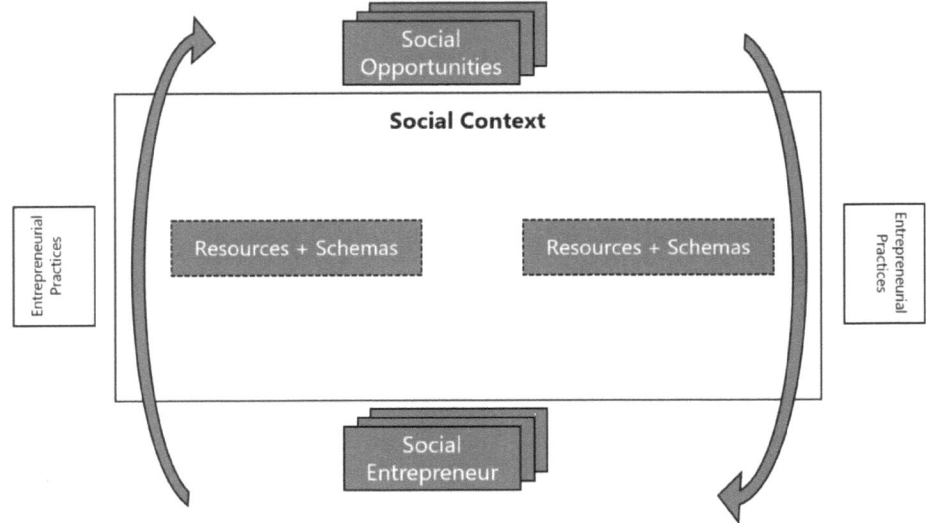

Figure 9: A structuration model for research on social entrepreneurship (based on Cajaiba-Santana, 2010, p. 102)

Cajaiba-Santana's (2010) recursive model of opportunity creation applies structuration theory to social entrepreneurship (Figure 9). Entrepreneurs are engaged in the ongoing creation and pursuit of opportunities. This cyclical pursuit ultimately alters structures. This study investigates various entrepreneurial approaches and differentiates them along several dimensions of proximity that will be introduced in the following chapter.

The Role of Proximity

Schumpeter's (1939) famous term "new combinations" describes innovation in today's most basic understanding. It implies not only that an innovation contains novelty but also that this novelty is created by the combination of resources and schemas that already exist. It follows that, in one way or another, proximity is a crucial enabling factor for combinations of any sort and thus for innovation. That is the reason why proximity has increasingly been investigated in the research on innovation (Boschma, 2005). Proximity of some sort is also implicit in the prominently used term "ecosystem" (Kadyrova, 2021), especially in the urban context. Spatial aspects of proximity also find relevance in the literature on clusters, territories, and localities in social innovation (Gerli et al., 2022; Moulaert et al., 2005; Tricarico et al., 2022; Van Dyck & Van Den Broeck, 2013). For social enterprises and nonprofit organizations in particular, the influence of spatial proximity in the sense of the community and culture of the place of operation is important (Mazzei, 2017).

Proximity research has roots in economic geography (Balland et al., 2022). It has established itself as an important area of the research on innovation since Boschma (2005) detailed the influence of spatial proximity and other forms of proximity. Specifically, he discussed four other dimensions: cognitive, organizational, social, and institutional proximity. One of the major scholarly insights in the field was that higher proximity does not generally increase innovative performance (Boschma, 2005; Boschma & Frenken, 2010). This is referred to as the proximity paradox. Lock-in, which results from a higher than optimal proximity and which is manifested in a lack of openness and flexibility, impedes the possibility of new combinations. In conclusion, there is an optimal point at which innovative performance is highest and after which more proximity will hinder innovative performance. The following paragraphs introduce the relevant dimensions of proximity and provide the theoretical basis for the analysis.

Cognitive proximity is defined as the degree of the shared knowledge base (Boschma, 2005). More similarity in the interpretation and evaluation of the world implies higher cognitive proximity (Presutti et al., 2011, p. 374). Social entrepreneurs, just like any other economic actors, are subject to bounded rationality (Boschma, 2005). Hence, knowledge can be widely different between individuals, but it can also overlap significantly. In relation to structuration theory, cognitive proximity can be regarded as the degree to which the schemas of actors align. A minimal shared knowledge base is necessary to the absorptive capacity for learning (Cohen & Levinthal, 1990). Despite the advantage of higher novelty for learning, there is a disadvantage of decreased mutual understanding (Wuyts et al., 2005). However, an overlap of knowledge to a large degree limits learning.

Social proximity refers to how closely individual agents are related to each other (Boschma, 2005). Higher social proximity is characterized by higher trust between individuals and a reduced danger of opportunistic behavior. Friendships, for example, are characterized by high social proximity. When agents develop close ties, their relation becomes embedded (Granovetter, 1985). Overembeddedness is characterized by a high social proximity that limits the entry of newcomers into a tight network of mutual acquaintance (Balland et al., 2015; Uzzi, 1997). Furthermore, social ties can decouple. This happens, for example, when two former employees of an organization retain their social ties after one leaves the organization. The decoupling leads to greater autonomy in the relationship (Grossetti, 2008).

Institutional proximity is defined as "the extent of shared norms, habits, rules and laws between economic agents" (Hansen, 2015, p. 1674). In contrast to social proximity and its focus on the micro level, it concerns the macro level (Boschma, 2005). The hybrid field of social entrepreneurship is becoming increasingly institutionalized (Balland et al., 2015; Glynn et al., 2020). For example, the benefit corporation is a legal form designated for hybrid organizations in the US (Rawhouser et al., 2015). The goal of SII programs is to induce an augmentation in participant's institutional proximity in relation to the field of social entrepreneurship. This alignment on an institutional level is hypothesized to facilitate sensemaking processes (Glynn et al., 2020).

Spatial proximity refers to the "physical distance between economic actors" (Boschma, 2005, p. 69). Spatial proximity is not necessary for learning because it can be substituted with other forms of proximity. In addition, digitalization has reduced the range of resources for which spatial proximity needs to be high. Nevertheless, many resources require proximity in a physical sense. These include, for example, the use of infrastructure, such as a coworking space in an SII. In addition to the lack of necessity for spatial proximity in learning, spatial proximity is also not sufficient to ensure learning because cognitive proximity needs to be present to some degree. The problem of lock-in has also been investigated in the context of spatial proximity, primarily in the business context (Ben Letaifa & Rabeau, 2013), and there is a lack of understanding of the dynamics of spatial proximity in the context of social entrepreneurship.

Organizational proximity is the least relevant in the context of this empirical study, because participants' learning processes were focused on the individual rather than organizational level. Organizational proximity was therefore excluded as a dimension of analysis.

Proximity research has moved toward a more dynamic approach in conceptualization, stressing the importance of assessing changes over time (Balland et al., 2015) and investigating the interrelations between different types of proximity (Huber, 2012). Studies have shown that it is easier to access more diverse knowledge when knowledge accumulation is facilitated by local relationships (Huber, 2012). For example, different institutional backgrounds can be overcome by spatial proximity (Ponds et al., 2007). The dimensions can also be substituted for each other (Hansen, 2015). Because structuration theory lacks a detailed consideration of proximity, applying the two in combination will be helpful for analyzing the SII of this case study.

Incubators and Proximity

Although incubators started appearing in the mid-20th century (Hausberg & Korreck, 2020), they first began to attract increased attention from researchers in the early 2000s (Phan et al., 2005). Most organizations conduct programs in a cyclical manner for cohorts of ventures selected based on specific criteria (Butz & Mrożewski, 2021; Yang, 2020). During the program, ventures receive support in the form of both human and nonhuman resources. Incubators aim to create contexts of resource munificence to reduce the fragility of newly founded organizations (Amezcua et al., 2013). For-profit organizations often take equity in supported ventures in exchange for their services.

Accelerators are not always clearly differentiated from incubators and offer similar services. The basis for their differentiation varies. Casasnovas and Bruno (2013) argue that accelerators focus on later-stage ventures with defined business models that aim to scale. Others propose that the length of the program is the differentiating factor, suggesting that accelerators generally use shorter programs to facilitate rapid growth, and they assume failure if startups are unable to grow rapidly (Mahmoud-Jouini et al., 2018).

Business incubators and accelerators have been thoroughly researched (Hackett & Dilts, 2004). Major research topics include elaborating typologies of the different programs, their potential impacts, and their processes (Hausberg & Korreck, 2020). The influence of proximity has been studied in the context of the processes of such programs (Schutjens & Kruger, 2020). Intermediary organizations generally attempt to reduce different dimensions of proximity internally and with external partners (Schepis, 2021; Villani et al., 2017). Cooper et al. (2012) showed that spatial proximity is central in incubators, since tacit knowledge is more accessible through spatial proximity, in contrast to explicit knowledge, which can be easily acquired in virtual environments (Cuvero et al., 2022). As the theory predicts, empirical studies have identified negative effects of both excessive and insufficient proximity. For example, a lack of mutual knowledge can lead to problems for learning (Cramton, 2001). In contrast, Mcadam and Marlow (2007) described how an excess in proximity has negative effects. In their study, excessively proximate participants moved "away from mutuality to protecting individuality and market share" (p. 374) due to the competitiveness of the environment.

Incubators specifically focusing on ventures with a social mission have not been extensively studied (Butz & Mrożewski, 2021; Sansone et al., 2020). The services they offer include training, mentoring, networking with partners and customers, networking with like-minded entrepreneurs, direct funding through seed capital, indirect funding through access to investors, and building awareness and credibility (Pandey et al., 2017). SIIs play a prominent role as intermediaries in social-innovation ecosystems (Ho & Yoon, 2022). Early evidence has suggested that social-impact accelerators have a causal effect on the emergence of nascent impact-oriented social ventures (Kher et al., 2022; Lall et al., 2020). However, there is a dearth of literature on how learning takes place and is influenced by proximity in SIIs. This study addresses this lack.

Through an increased understanding of these dynamics, the processes of innovation targeting systems change can be differentiated and transferred to different contexts.

Methodology

Research Design, Context, and Case Selection

The case-study method is the recommended method for studying phenomena that are not well understood. It is suited for investigating processes and how questions (Yin, 2018). Additionally, case studies are apt for theory building related to complex processes and phenomena that are hard to measure (Gehman et al., 2018).

This study has been conducted as a holistic single case study. This approach is justified on the basis of its revelatory nature, as SII programs are not publicly accessible. The program was conducted by the Social Innovation Lab and focused on nascent social ventures. It was determined to be suitable based on several factors. First, the chosen program is embedded in a rich ecosystem. The Social Innovation Lab is one of the organizational units of Grünhof in Freiburg, Germany. The organization conducts several incubation and acceleration programs. For example, there are other programs for established nonprofit organizations and technology ventures. It has also been able to secure public funding. Another reason for selecting this program was that its facilities were within a reasonable travel distance from the researcher's location for data collection. Repeated access to the facilities is central because learning processes are not easily observed.

The program observed for this study was conducted from March 2022 to July 2022. The participants were selected by a jury of two employees and one executive from one of the funding organizations in January 2022. The choice was made based on six selection criteria (Table 6). Applications were received through an online form. A total of 39 applications were received, of which eight organizations, consisting of twelve individual participants, were invited to participate in the program. Nine out of twelve participants had a background in social work. The program was composed of six modules and one closing event. Each module had a dedicated topic and ranged from understanding systems change to financing and communication. The projects were pitched at a closing event with external visitors. As stated in its annual report, the vision of the Social Innovation Lab is the creation of a society worth living in for all, where social challenges are a motivator for collaboration. The investigated program is funded by a German foundation and a lottery. Grants are requested yearly for the implementation of the program. The program did not provide direct funding for participants. Apart from funding, all other major categories of support typically offered by similar programs were provided, including coworking space as well as access to mentorship and a broad network (Pandey et al., 2017). The activities of the organization also align with the roles of other intermediaries in social entrepreneurship ecosystems (Ho & Yoon, 2022).

Selection Criteria
Clarity of concept
Potential of leverage through program
Focus on relevant social problem
Scalability
Novelty of social innovation
Entrepreneurial approach

Table 6: Selection criteria for the program

Data Collection and Analysis

Data collection for the case was based on multiple data types and separated into two phases. The first phase lasted the duration of the program and was inductive. The goal was to develop a thorough understanding of the program and how it is embedded in the ecosystem. Data was collected through ethnographic participation during multiple field visits (Spradley, 1980). Field notes were taken in four modules. Each module lasted a day. During this phase, additional documentation was received from employees at the SII (Table 7).

Source	Type of data	Quantity	Use in the analysis
Primary data: interviews	Semi-structured interviews - February 2022 (1) - March 2022 (2) - May 2022 (3) - September 2022 (4) - October 2022 (3) - December 2022 (2)	9 h and 20 min of interviews (3 via Zoom call, 10 at social-innovation lab, 2 at participant location)	Analyzed according to Gioia methodology
Primary data: ethnographic participation	Field notes from field visits - March 2022 – Module 1 & 2 - May 2022 – Module 3 & 4	4 days during modules resulting in 3 pages of field notes (.pdf)	Support and triangulation of evidence from interviews
Secondary data: documentation	- Annual report 2020 & 2021 - Participant profiles - Emails from SII - Program applications - Written evaluations of applications - News article - Presentation and teaching material - Recordings of introductory discussions - Telegram chat messages in two chats (March – September)	- 32 pages (.pdf) - 8 pages (.pdf) - 19 - 39 applicant-answers (.xls) - Comments from 3 jurors on 39 applicants (.xls) - 1 page (.pdf) - 307 pages (.jpg, .pdf, .xls) - 3 h 15 min - >300 messages	Support and triangulation of evidence from interviews

Table 7: Data sources

Access was granted to the documentation of the selection process and the written evaluations. Furthermore, access to all the emails between program employees and participants was provided. These included all the presentations and further resources from the program. In addition to the field notes and documentation, semi-structured interviews were used to access the knowledge of the participants. This method belongs to the most widespread interview techniques. It provides some structure for what topics should be covered but also grants the researcher the flexibility to focus the conversation on issues important to answering the research questions (Brinkmann, 2013). The interview guide followed Dinca-Panaitescu's (2020) two-leveled approach for studying social-innovation labs. The first level relates to the activities of participants, the second to the larger goals of systems change. For the purpose of this study, a middle level relating to the social-innovation ecosystem was added, so the interview guide covered three topics: 1) the relationship of SII employees with participants in the program, 2) the embedding of the program within the organization and ecosystem, and 3) the role of the program in contributing to systems change. Interviews were conducted with two employees of the SII organization and four participants in the program.

The second phase of data collection lasted from the closing event of the program to the end of 2022 (Figure 10). Data collection took place only through semi-structured interviews. Since the interviews were based on an abductive approach, theoretical considerations guided the development of the interview questions and the interview guide (Rubin & Rubin, 2012). Structuration theory and the different dimensions of proximity were determined to be of significant importance. Structuration theory provides insights into the role of resources and schemas in the learning process. Differences among cognitive, social, institutional, and spatial proximity formed a further background for investigating the dynamics of that process. A total of nine interviews were conducted in phase two; all of them were with participants in the program. The interviews were transcribed shortly after they had taken place and then analyzed to identify further questions. A focus was placed on open-ended questions (Rubin & Rubin, 2012). The interviews lasted 38 minutes on average, with a range of 26 minutes to 51 minutes. The length of the interviews differed depending on the amount of information available from other data sources on the participants. Interviewees were chosen through purposeful sampling. All but two of the interviews took place face-to-face. The majority of the in-person interviews were conducted in the facilities of the SII organization. Data collection through interviews was stopped when the new data did not contribute to the research question. The accuracy of an assessment of descriptive information was confirmed by the participants (Table 8, appendix). Participant observation, documentation, and semi-structured interviews allowed the triangulation of the data (Spradley, 1980).

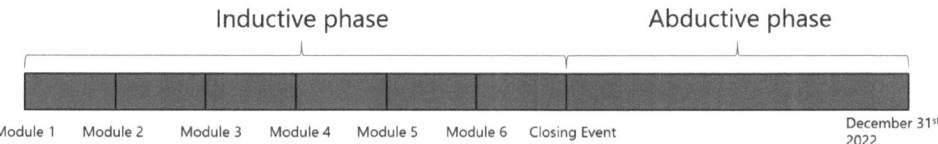

Figure 10: Phases of data collection (own illustration)

The data analysis followed the Gioia method (Gioia et al., 2013). It empowers the researcher to develop new understandings in a rigorous and systematic manner. It is particularly well suited to connecting informant-based understandings with theory (Magnani & Gioia, 2023). Several rounds of descriptive and open coding were conducted to identify how participants learn about hybrid organizing. Numerous first-order concepts emerged. By exploring differences and similarities, the first-order concepts were aggregated but kept in the informants' terms. The results were also shown to and discussed with the manager of the program to confirm the accuracy of the findings.

Relevant documents, websites, and media reports enabled further triangulation. Patterns in the first-order concepts were then further aggregated to second-order themes. During this phase, emphasis was placed on developing themes that were congruent with the theoretical background of the study for the purpose of developing a theoretical contribution. From the second-order themes, two aggregate dimensions emerged.

Findings

Through the process of iteration between data and theory, a data structure was developed that describes the relationship of the program participants to the SII program. The model differentiates between two general approaches: proximity augmentation and proximity moderation. Different dimensions of proximity were augmented when motivation was built through resources, when schemas were redefined and internalized, and a resource repository was constructed. By contrast, participants also moderated proximity by limiting identification, valuing previous connections, and protecting personal well-being (Figure 11). These dynamics will be elaborated in this section.

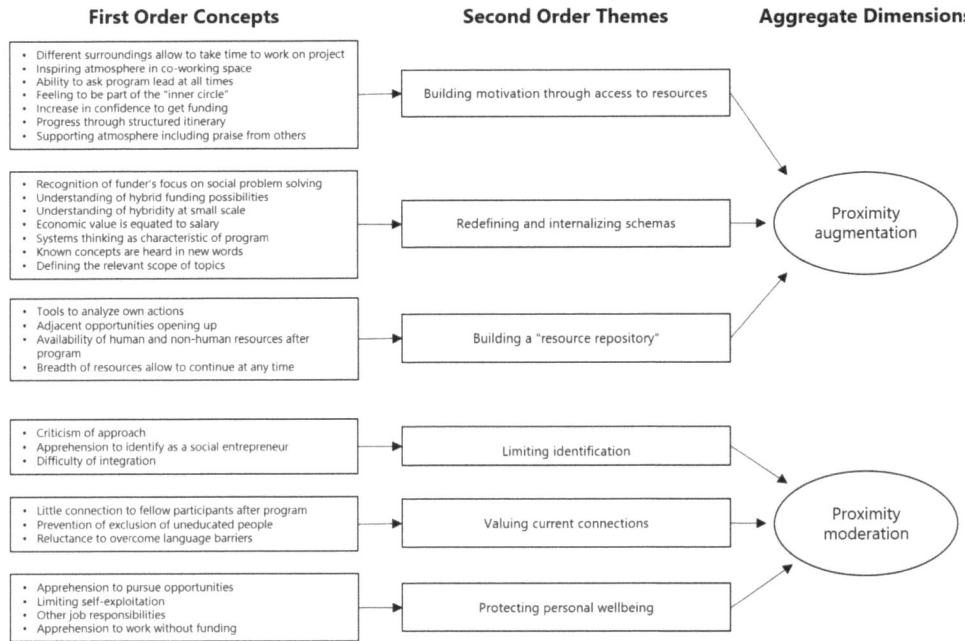

Figure 11: Data structure (own illustration)

Proximity Augmentation

Building Motivation through Resources

Building motivation through resources describes instances where participants augmented proximity. The SII provided significant services in the form of nonhuman resources, such as physical infrastructure. Within the facilities, a designated office space was offered specifically for the program participants and alumni. During the program, its use was free of charge. The temporary nature of the facilities as a meeting place avoids high sunk costs (Rychen & Zimmermann, 2008). After the program, the space could be utilized for a small monthly fee, ensuring long-term availability of workspace. The availability of office space was generally considered important by the participants. It served as a major motivator for working on the development of the ventures. This buffering effect, which allows organizations to isolate themselves and develop without direct exposure to environmental threats, has been identified in incubators before (Amezcua et al., 2013). Buffering refers to a moderation of proximity to the general environment and a consequent augmentation of spatial proximity to the SII.

Overall, these resources, as well as the structure of the program itself, provided motivation in the face of an endeavor that was at times perceived as overwhelming. For example, after the modules the program structure provided homework that asked the participants to complete specific tasks. As explained by participant 4 from venture C:

"You always had the feeling that you were advancing step by step."

In addition to nonhuman resources, human resources also played a significant role in building motivation. Social proximity significantly increased over the span of the program. Participants mentioned the possibility of asking the program lead questions at any time as a significant benefit. They highly valued the feedback from both the SII employees and their fellow participants. The atmosphere within the facilities was consistently described as inspiring and motivating. The network of entrepreneurial activity aided in overcoming hesitations when addressing challenging problems. Encouragement and support from others also boosted confidence in securing funding. Advice on specific topics was available, for example, through email or messaging applications. This meant that support from others was accessible remotely as well. Digital communication technology even facilitated the sense of belonging to an inner circle, as explained by participant 1:

"[...] but also to be in the Telegram group and to get the news about what NGOs or organizations are looking for [...]"

Redefining and Internalizing Schemas

Institutional and cognitive proximity are specifically relevant in the process of redefining and internalizing schemas. The explicit goal of the program makes this apparent. It aims to familiarize participants with the social entrepreneurship ecosystem and to establish a shared vocabulary. The modules were structured as input sessions and work sessions to facilitate this process. During the input sessions, concepts and theoretical knowledge were presented that guided the individual work sessions and activities between modules. The purpose of the input sessions was to bridge gaps in cognitive proximity. For instance, the first module focused on the concept of systems change and on expanding participants' perspectives on the social problem they were aiming to solve. A theory frequently mentioned as a framework for transformative change was that of a multilevel perspective (Avelino et al., 2019), which recognizes transitions occurring at the reinforcing levels of landscape, regime, and niches (Geels, 2005). This clearly shows that absorptive capacity for learning was enhanced through augmenting cognitive proximity.

Furthermore, the program introduced social entrepreneurship and the integration of social and economic goals as central schemas. The schemas prescribed by a social entrepreneurial approach often differed from those of a social work approach, which was the background for nine of the twelve participants. Throughout the program, participants became familiar with a more hybrid understanding of organizational activity. For example, social work prescribes conducting organizational activities in a participatory manner by involving people in the development of a product or in the provision of a service. Participant 6 from venture D explained how the program shifted their perspective toward an approach aimed at a higher efficiency as prescribed by an economic logic:

> "Probably also because we used to see it in a classic social work manner because of our background as social workers. We involve people who build it with us or other possibilities. And that has gone away more and more. The more modules we have visited here, the less it was in the end this classic social work, up to the point that we now say that no one helps build it, no one will come into contact with it in any other way."

Most participants had limited knowledge of social entrepreneurship (see appendix), so the program also redefined participants' notions of the field itself. This led some participants to augment their perceived institutional proximity to social entrepreneurship and strengthen their personal identification as social entrepreneurs, as explained by participant 11 from venture G:

> "Yes, I just did not know that much about what it is exactly or somehow imagined something different. But it is also that there can be individual social entrepreneurs. [...] So I do not have to be a [large] organization to do something like that [...]."

The complementarity of social and financial aspects in organizational development was emphasized during the program. This complementarity was recognized in specific instances. For example, the program noted the significance of a clear and relevant social mission to securing external funding. It was also acknowledged that providing social services has a monetary value for certain stakeholders. However, rather than emphasizing wealth creation and unlimited growth, economic success was associated with sustaining the organization and being able to provide a salary that covers living expenses. Furthermore, the possibility of establishing multiple organizations with both for-profit and nonprofit legal forms was suggested. This expanded the range of funding opportunities to include private and third-sector funders. The redefinition and internalization of schemas were facilitated by social proximity, particularly when the knowledge was more implicit or tacit. Social proximity, in turn, was often positively influenced by higher spatial proximity.

The participants' self-identification as social entrepreneurs remained low until the end of the data collection (see appendix). The reason for this is not a lack of willingness to identify as such. Most participants felt that their efforts were not successful enough at this stage for them to be able to identify as social entrepreneurs.

Building a "Resource Repository"

Nonhuman and human resources often did not have immediate value when they were first offered. Due to the relatively short duration of the program for participants, resources were accumulated. This allowed access at a later time and was particularly relevant for participants in the early stages of organizational development. For example, former participants benefited from the ability to utilize office space at a low price even after the program, as alluded to above. Human resources also remained accessible through the network, as explained by participant 6 from venture D:

"Once in a while you can also ask someone during the founding process and say *hey, come, let's sit together for a day, let's tackle this topic.*"

The availability of structures and a repository of resources were crucial, particularly in phases characterized by a low level of motivation. The observations during phase one of data collection revealed that early-stage social entrepreneurs need to adapt their strategy repeatedly within a short period of time (Kirtley & O'Mahony, 2023). Human and nonhuman resources in a resource repository provide the opportunity to pivot in a more informed way. In these cases, progress could be greatly accelerated.

In many cases, these resources were available in digital format, which makes them particularly flexible in their use. The resources also included models and templates that participants were introduced to during the input sessions of the modules. One example is the social-business-model canvas (Nair, 2022). As participant 7 from venture E explained:

"I think it has given me a lot of ideas for analyzing my approach and my actions better."

There were variations in the usefulness of different resources. A financial planning template was only utilized by one venture before the end of data collection. The other ventures were not sufficiently developed organizationally to make use of the template.

Furthermore, the significance of human resources to opportunity creation was evident. This took place through established and enduring social proximity with various individuals in the SII's network. Participants could direct specific questions to individuals possessing the knowledge to solve a problem. For example, a participant from venture F inquired about trademark filings and accounting services and received direct responses or personal referrals from the SII employees. Social proximity facilitated the funneling of opportunities, even though social relations were decoupled to a large degree at the end of the program.

In business contexts characterized by rivalry, the literature indicates that spatial proximity decreases social proximity (Ben Letaifa & Rabeau, 2013). However, in this SII program, where competition was only minimally present, spatial proximity significantly increased social proximity. Furthermore, the SII environment was not considered a formal institutional setting by the participants, so it did not hinder spontaneous social proximity, and excessive embeddedness was not a major concern.

Proximity Moderation

Limiting Identification

Depending on their educational background, participants approached the program with different schemas. This difference in the institutional background of the participants and that of the SII led to an environment of institutional complexity. As mentioned in the context of the redefinition of schemas, the principles of social work and the emerging field of social entrepreneurship were not always compatible (Greenwood et al., 2011). This resulted in specific instances when opposing field-level logics created tensions. For instance, some participants considered the overall pace of activity too fast. Participants with a social work background felt that this emphasis on speed was excessively aligned with a business logic. They questioned whether the program could not have been conducted over a longer time period. The increase in spatial proximity amplified their feelings of discomfort, as expressed by participant 7 from venture E:

"At the beginning, I thought, *wow, in what kind of a world did I end up here?* It was peculiar somehow."

Rather than fully adopting a new logic, participants built on their existing social context and selectively incorporated elements from the new context (Pache & Santos, 2013). The reluctance of many participants to identify as social entrepreneurs was, for the most part, not due to a lack of desire to do so. Instead, it stemmed from the low maturity level and lack of professionalization of their organizations, which made them hesitant to embrace the identity of a social entrepreneur. This hesitation was also influenced by differences in the meaning of entrepreneurship in the German context. As participant 12 highlights, the literal translation of entrepreneurship to German ("Unternehmertum") carries a more bureaucratic and hard-nosed connotation:

"I then always ask myself in my head, would I now call myself an entrepreneur, or isn't that something that has to do with capitalism and raking in money and so on?"

Furthermore, as highlighted by Grohs et al. (2017), the German third sector maintains close connections with the public sector. This poses challenges for early-stage organizations seeking to integrate into this network. The significant disparity between entrepreneurial practices and social organizations in this context makes it more challenging to reconcile these two aspects.

Valuing Previous Connections

Participants not only gained access to new resources through the program but also utilized their preexisting resources. While the program provided a significant amount of nonhuman resources, participants relied on human resources from their existing connections. As a result, social proximity to the SII was limited since maintaining a high level of social proximity with one group necessitates sacrificing social proximity with another group (Uzzi, 1997). Participant 11 from venture G explains the problems of this trade-off:

"Of course, I always make sure that I do not exclude people by using words that might scare them off and they think, *oh God, what is that?* Especially if they are not highly educated."

In their predominantly German-speaking work environment, the terminology used in the field of social entrepreneurship posed a barrier to connecting with their target group. Thus, to maintain proximity to their previous connections, they moderated their proximity to the SII. This trade-off was also manifested in a moderation of social and spatial proximity over time. On average, participants' presence at the coworking space decreased after the program. With no additional official gatherings or events, other interactions among the participants diminished as well.

Protecting Personal Well-being

The institutional logics in the fields of both social work and social entrepreneurship are influenced by resource scarcity and the consequent need to maximize the utilization of these limited resources. None of the participants were able to earn an income from their venture activities that would have provided a sustainable livelihood, so committing to a newly established venture without funding entailed significant risks to their personal finances. Participant 11 from venture G expressed notable caution:

"[A job in the social sector] is already so badly paid anyway. Especially if you are a person who cares about social impact. That is also the case for permanent employees. This is really an issue, and you have to take care of yourself."

Because of these circumstances, the majority of the participants in the SII program engaged in part-time work both during and after the program. This practice of hybrid entrepreneurship is also common among traditional business ventures (Demir et al., 2022). While business entrepreneurs may earn more in their entrepreneurial venture than in their salaried job, this is an unlikely scenario in the context of social entrepreneurship (Schulz et al., 2017). Despite their modest goal of covering their own salaries, achieving this objective remained a significant challenge for all the participants. Their part-time work required substantial resources and moderated their proximity to the SII in all the dimensions of proximity.

Limited resources were also evident in other aspects. For instance, the spatial proximity of the program was crucial due to the costs involved in participating. The time and financial resources required for traveling to another city would have posed a significant barrier for most of the participants. The scarcity of resources also led to a reluctance to pursue opportunities. Participant 1 from venture A expressed this concern:

"Do I really want to become self-employed and just found something? What does that mean for my social insurance and everything?"

In addition to financial implications, there were potential consequences for the participants' physical and mental well-being, including a risk of burnout. Participant 9 from venture F explained previous experience in this regard as follows:

"When I have done too much volunteering, I simply get frustrated, and that does not work in the long run. It must also sustain you somehow."

The strong intrinsic motivation to address a social problem and the resulting sense of responsibility can lead to negative outcomes for some entrepreneurs (Wei et al., 2015), so they institute a self-imposed moderation of proximity to protect their mental well-being.

Discussion

Key Findings and Contribution

This study laid out the learning process of participants in an SII program. The proposed model is based on Cajaiba-Santana (2010) application of structuration theory to opportunity creation in social entrepreneurship (Figure 12). In addition, the study used the two essential mechanisms of proximity augmentation and proximity moderation to describe the interactions of the participants in the SII program. Proximity was augmented by building motivation through access to resources. Further, resources supplied by the program provided participants with the opportunity to construct a resource repository. A repository allowed participants to access resources after the program had concluded. This process was facilitated by the augmentation of spatial and social proximity. Schemas were internalized and redefined, leading to an augmentation of proximity in the cognitive and institutional dimensions. Proximity moderation occurred in participants' limited self-identification as social entrepreneurs. Moreover, social and institutional proximity to previous connections was maintained. This also led to proximity moderation in the cognitive and spatial dimensions. Further, participants felt that their personal well-being was jeopardized, which led to efforts to protect it and, consequently, to proximity moderation. These dynamics make apparent the oppositional nature of augmentation and moderation. An increase in augmentation implies a decrease in moderation. Nevertheless, both augmentation and moderation occur concurrently and in different dimensions of proximity (Figure 12).

The transfer of resources was easily observable and was the most obvious aspect of the support provided by the SII program to the participants. This has been stressed repeatedly in the literature (Amezcua et al., 2013). Schemas, on the other hand, have not been a focus of attention. Thus, one contribution of this study lies in pointing out instances of the successful transfer of schemas to participants. The empirical analysis shows that schemas were equally important to resources in the process of venture development.

As predicted in the literature on proximity, participants evaded the lock-in effect of excessive proximity (Boschma, 2005). This process, termed proximity moderation, was described in detail in this study. The empirical evidence for this mechanism contributes to the literature on proximity. Positive effects of proximity augmentation on venture development were observed repeatedly. In addition, negative effects of insufficient proximity on the learning process were observed as well. They were salient in all the dimensions of proximity. For example, some participants rarely used the coworking space. This lack in spatial proximity led to a moderation of social, institutional, and cognitive proximity as well. In terms of social aspects, for example, participants were not able to make the necessary social connections to develop their network because they were not physically present at the coworking space. This effect of the moderation of spatial proximity on other proximity dimensions exemplifies their interrelatedness. This study also contributed to structuration theory and the application of structuration theory in social entrepreneurship. By answering the call for an application of structuration theory in a longitudinal case study (Cajaiba-Santana, 2010), this investigation has provided further advances in the empirical application of this theory. Most importantly, the knowledgeability of agents, an important aspect in structuration theory, was evident in their purposeful actions to moderate and augment proximity.

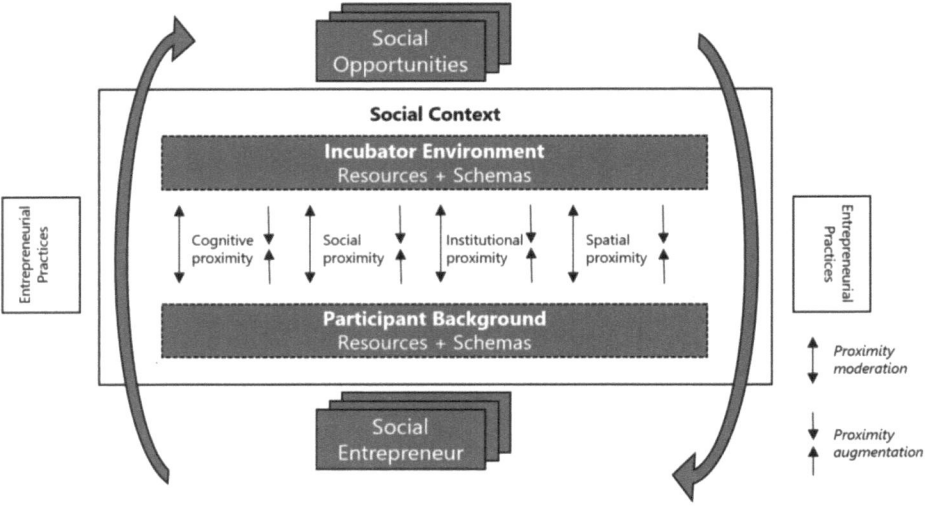

Figure 12: Model of dynamic proximity in an SII program (based on Cajaiba-Santana, 2010)

The practical implications of this study are manifold. First, it suggests that heterogeneity of SII participants should be limited because excessive heterogeneity can limit learning and innovation. For participants to profit most from an environment of resource munificence, the services should be targeted to a more specific group. This concerns the stage of organizational development of the ventures as well as the background of participants. Assessing and understanding participants' backgrounds and their proximity at the beginning and end of the program are significant measures for assessing their learning process and the overall success of the program. Recommendations for optimal proximity cannot be given independently of the context and organization. For example, the country-specific institutional context in Germany had a large influence on the SII environment and the activities of the participants. Mair and Rathert (2020) found that social enterprises in Germany perceive lower growth opportunities than social enterprises in Sweden or the UK. They also found a lack of financing to be one of the most significant barriers. These factors are important to consider when transferring findings from this study to other contexts. Particularly in terms of hybridity, which emerged as a central theme in the program, an SII should be limited in terms of the relative importance of economic and social aspects (Shepherd et al., 2019). There should be an emphasis on combining social and economic goals and the specific trade-offs involved. These factors influence the structure, content, and timeline of SII programs. Overall, theory and the empirical evidence from this study speak to the importance of achieving a balance that avoids both excessive as well as insufficient proximity.

Furthermore, this study provides many implications for social work practices. It observed social work practitioners outside of their salaried job. The institutional logics of social work greatly influenced the SII program, because the majority of the participants had a social work background. For example, organizational activities were influenced by their values of participation and their attention to human needs. These logics influenced the development of the ventures.

In addition to the influence of the institutional logics of social work on the ventures, the incubator environment also affected the participants' jobs in social work. Most of the participants were not able to earn an income from the ventures and continued in their jobs. In the business environment, entrepreneurs engaged in the development of an organization often transfer their innovative capability to their salaried jobs (Demir et al., 2022). The same is expected in the context of SII programs. This means that SII programs can have far-reaching effects beyond the specific venture.

Conclusions: Limitations and Future Research

Some of the limitations of this study originate from the methodological approach. The case-study method entails several methodological limitations. Even though clearer procedures have been developed in recent years, critics have pointed out that there is not an established systematic methodology for case studies, so evaluating their quality is more difficult compared to other research methods (Yin, 2018). Further, the generalizability of case studies has been questioned. However, this case study aspires to be transferable, not generalizable (Gioia, 2021). Despite differences in the context of social entrepreneurship between countries, there are also similarities (Defourny & Nyssens, 2017; Kerlin, 2010), which can make the findings from one case study transferable to a variety of contexts. The goal of this study was to expand on theory in a nascent research area. These theories may be tested through multiple case studies or quantitative research methods at a later stage (Flyvbjerg, 2006). Finally, a further limitation of this single case study was the small number of participants, a limitation that could be skewed in a variety of directions.

Future research avenues concern the assessment of performance of SIIs. A differentiated view of SIIs' support mechanisms has been called for to better identify their contributions to organizational survival (Amezcua et al., 2013). Proximity paradox provides a lens for assessing success. This study provided initial advances in its application.

Further research should also be conducted to assess the financial stability of organizations conducting SII programs and the types of funding they draw on. Securing funds for an SII program represents a great difficulty in implementing them. Since the services are provided to participants on a cost-free basis, the funding is usually secured by a mix of philanthropic and public funds as well as earned income. A better understanding of how to develop long-term relationships with funders would help practitioners implement SII programs. Further, the potential of earned income in this context could help SII organizations become more resilient. Optimal pricing is a challenge and needs to be further investigated (Young et al., 2010). Regarding social work practice, investigating the transfer of knowledge to program participants' jobs would be a fruitful research avenue. The detailed effects of this transfer are unknown. For example, it would be interesting to investigate whether social work practitioners who participate in an SII program become less risk-averse and more innovative. This would extend the field of hybrid entrepreneurship to social entrepreneurs and their employment in social work.

Venture name (anonymized)	Legal status (31 December 2022)	Participant (anonymized)	Other job responsibilities (31 December 2022)	Background	Presence at coworking space during program	Importance of geographical proximity of program	Identification as social entrepreneur	Degree of familiarity with social entrepreneurship terminology before program	Interviews
Venture A	Not yet incorporated	P1	90%	Social work	10	High	Low	Medium	Phase 2
Venture B	GmbH	P2	70%	Social work	15	High	High	Medium	Phase 2
		P3	60%	Social work	10	High	Low	Low	Phase 1
Venture C	Not yet incorporated	P4	Maternity leave	Social work	10	High	Low	Low	Phase 2
	Not yet incorporated	P5	50%	Social work	30	Medium	Low	Low	Phase 1
Venture D		P6	60%	Social work	30	Medium	Low	Low	Phase 2
Venture E	Project by existing cooperative	P7	50%	Social work	1	High	No	Low	Phase 2
		P8	70%	Academia and sports	15	High	High	High	Phase 1 and 2
Venture F	Association	P9	80%	Academia and sports	15	High	Unsure	Medium	Phase 2
	Not incorporated yet	P10	100%	Social work	0	High	No	Low	Phase 2
Venture G		P11	60%	Social work	0	High	No	Low	Phase 2
Venture H	Association	P12	50%	Academia and third sector	10	Medium	No	Low	Phase 1

Table 8: Descriptive information on participants

References

Amezcua, A. S., Grimes, M. G., Bradley, S. W., & Wiklund, J. (2013). Organizational Sponsorship and Founding Environments: A Contingency View on the Survival of Business-Incubated Firms, 1994–2007. *Academy of Management Journal, 56*(6), 1628-1654.

Avelino, F., Wittmayer, J. M., Pel, B., Weaver, P., Dumitru, A., Haxeltine, A., Kemp, R., Jørgensen, M. S., Bauler, T., Ruijsink, S., & O'Riordan, T. (2019). Transformative social innovation and (dis)empowerment. *Technological Forecasting and Social Change, 145*, 195-206.

Balland, P.-A., Boschma, R., & Frenken, K. (2015). Proximity and Innovation: From Statics to Dynamics. *Regional Studies, 49*(6), 907-920.

Balland, P.-A., Boschma, R., & Frenken, K. (2022). Proximity, innovation and networks: a concise review and some next steps. In *Handbook of Proximity Relations*. Cheltenham, UK: Edward Elgar Publishing.

Bartunek, J. M. (1984). Changing Interpretive Schemes and Organizational Restructuring: The Example of a Religious Order. *Administrative Science Quarterly, 29*(3), 355-372.

Ben Letaifa, S., & Rabeau, Y. (2013). Too close to collaborate? How geographic proximity could impede entrepreneurship and innovation. *Journal of Business Research, 66*(10), 2071-2078.

Boschma, R. (2005). Proximity and Innovation: A Critical Assessment. *Regional Studies, 39*(1), 61-74.

Boschma, R., & Frenken, K. (2010). The spatial evolution of innovation networks: a proximity perspective. In *The handbook of evolutionary economic geography*. Edward Elgar Publishing.

Brinkmann, S. (2013). *Qualitative interviewing*. New York: Oxford University Press.

Butz, H., & Mrożewski, M. J. (2021). The Selection Process and Criteria of Impact Accelerators. An Exploratory Study. *Sustainability, 13*(12).

Cajaiba-Santana, G. (2010). Socially constructed opportunities in social entrepreneurship: a structuration model. In *Handbook of Research on Social Entrepreneurship* (pp. 88-106). Cheltenham, UK: Edward Elgar Publishing.

Cajaiba-Santana, G. (2014). Social innovation: Moving the field forward. A conceptual framework. *Technological Forecasting and Social Change, 82*, 42-51.

Casasnovas, G., & Bruno, A. V. (2013). Scaling Social Ventures: An Exploratory Study of Social Incubators and Accelerators. *Journal of Management for Global Sustainability, 1*(2), 173-197.

Cohen, W. M., & Levinthal, D. A. (1990). Absorptive Capacity: A New Perspective on Learning and Innovation. *Administrative Science Quarterly, 35*(1), 128-152.

Cooper, C. E., Hamel, S. A., & Connaughton, S. L. (2012). Motivations and obstacles to networking in a university business incubator. *The Journal of Technology Transfer, 37*(4), 433-453.

Cramton, C. D. (2001). The Mutual Knowledge Problem and Its Consequences for Dispersed Collaboration. *Organization Science, 12*(3), 346-371.

Cuvero, M., Granados, M. L., Pilkington, A., & Evans, R. (2022). Start-ups' use of knowledge spillovers for product innovation: the influence of entrepreneurial ecosystems and virtual platforms. *R&D Management, n/a*(n/a).

Defourny, J., & Nyssens, M. (2017). Fundamentals for an International Typology of Social Enterprise Models. *VOLUNTAS: International Journal of Voluntary and Nonprofit Organizations, 28*(6), 2469-2497.

Demir, C., Werner, A., Kraus, S., & Jones, P. (2022). Hybrid entrepreneurship: a systematic literature review. *Journal of Small Business & Entrepreneurship, 34*(1), 29-52.

Dinca-Panaitescu, M. (2020). Dancing between 'zoom in' and 'zoom out' perspectives to evaluate Social Innovation Labs. *Canadian Journal of Program Evaluation, 35*(2).

Domanski, D., Howaldt, J., & Kaletka, C. (2019). A comprehensive concept of social innovation and its implications for the local context – on the growing importance of social innovation ecosystems and infrastructures. *European Planning Studies, 28*, 1-21.

Dorado, S., & Ventresca, M. J. (2013). Crescive entrepreneurship in complex social problems: Institutional conditions for entrepreneurial engagement. *Journal of Business Venturing, 28*(1), 69-82.

European Commission. (2021). *Social Economy Action Plan*. Retrieved 27 February 2024 from https://ec.europa.eu/social/main.jsp?catId=1537&langId=en

Fahrenwald, C., Kolleck, N., Schröer, A., & Truschkat, I. (2021). Editorial: "Social Innovation in Education" [Editorial]. *Frontiers in Education, 6*.

Geels, F. W. (2005). Processes and patterns in transitions and system innovations: Refining the co-evolutionary multi-level perspective. *Technological Forecasting and Social Change, 72*(6), 681-696.

Gehman, J., Glaser, V. L., Eisenhardt, K. M., Gioia, D., Langley, A., & Corley, K. G. (2018). Finding Theory–Method Fit: A Comparison of Three Qualitative Approaches to Theory Building. *Journal of Management Inquiry, 27*(3), 284-300.

Gerli, F., Calderini, M., & Chiodo, V. (2022). An ecosystemic model for the technological development of social entrepreneurship: exploring clusters of social innovation. *European Planning Studies, 30*(10), 1962-1984.

Giddens, A. (1986). *The constitution of society: Outline of the theory of structuration.* Cambridge: Polity.

Gioia, D. (2021). A Systematic Methodology for Doing Qualitative Research. *The Journal of Applied Behavioral Science, 57*(1), 20-29.

Gioia, D. A., Corley, K. G., & Hamilton, A. L. (2013). Seeking Qualitative Rigor in Inductive Research: Notes on the Gioia Methodology. *Organizational Research Methods, 16*(1), 15-31.

Glynn, M. A., Hood, E. A., & Innis, B. D. (2020). Taking hybridity for granted: Institutionalization and hybrid identification. In *Organizational hybridity: Perspectives, processes, promises* (Vol. 69, pp. 53-72). Emerald Publishing Limited.

Granovetter, M. (1985). Economic Action and Social Structure: The Problem of Embeddedness. *American Journal of Sociology, 91*(3), 481-510.

Greenwood, R., Raynard, M., Kodeih, F., Micelotta, E. R., & Lounsbury, M. (2011). Institutional Complexity and Organizational Responses. *The Academy of Management Annals, 5*(1), 317-371.

Grohs, S., Schneiders, K., & Heinze, R. G. (2017). Outsiders and Intrapreneurs: The Institutional Embeddedness of Social Entrepreneurship in Germany. *VOLUNTAS: International Journal of Voluntary and Nonprofit Organizations, 28*(6), 2569-2591.

Grossetti, M. (2008). Proximities and Embedding Effects. *European Planning Studies, 16*(5), 629-642.

Hackett, S. M., & Dilts, D. M. (2004). A Systematic Review of Business Incubation Research. *The Journal of Technology Transfer, 29*(1), 55-82.

Hansen, T. (2015). Substitution or Overlap? The Relations between Geographical and Non-spatial Proximity Dimensions in Collaborative Innovation Projects. *Regional Studies, 49*(10), 1672-1684.

Hausberg, J. P., & Korreck, S. (2020). Business incubators and accelerators: a co-citation analysis-based, systematic literature review. *The Journal of Technology Transfer, 45*(1), 151-176.

Ho, J.-Y., & Yoon, S. (2022). Ambiguous roles of intermediaries in social entrepreneurship: The case of social innovation system in South Korea. *Technological Forecasting and Social Change*, *175*, 121324.

Huber, F. (2012). On the Role and Interrelationship of Spatial, Social and Cognitive Proximity: Personal Knowledge Relationships of R&D Workers in the Cambridge Information Technology Cluster. *Regional Studies*, *46*(9), 1169-1182.

Jarzabkowski, P. (2008). Shaping Strategy as a Structuration Process. *The Academy of Management Journal*, *51*(4), 621-650.

Kadyrova, A. (2021). Exploring Structures of Urban Social Innovation Ecosystems: Cases of Manchester, Utrecht, Stockholm, Sofia and Budapest. *Journal of Social Entrepreneurship*, 1-23.

Kerlin, J. A. (2010). A Comparative Analysis of the Global Emergence of Social Enterprise. *VOLUNTAS: International Journal of Voluntary and Nonprofit Organizations*, *21*(2), 162-179.

Kher, R., Yang, S., & Newbert, S. L. (2022). Accelerating emergence: the causal (but contextual) effect of social impact accelerators on nascent for-profit social ventures. *Small Business Economics*.

Kirtley, J., & O'Mahony, S. (2023). What is a pivot? Explaining when and how entrepreneurial firms decide to make strategic change and pivot. *Strategic Management Journal*, *44*(1), 197-230.

Labianca, G., Gray, B., & Brass, D. J. (2000). A Grounded Model of Organizational Schema Change During Empowerment. *Organization Science*, *11*(2), 235-257.

Lall, S. A., Chen, L.-W., & Roberts, P. W. (2020). Are we accelerating equity investment into impact-oriented ventures? *World Development*, *131*, 104952.

Magnani, G., & Gioia, D. (2023). Using the Gioia Methodology in international business and entrepreneurship research. *International Business Review*, *32*(2), 102097.

Mahmoud-Jouini, S. B., Duvert, C., & Esquirol, M. (2018). Key Factors in Building a Corporate Accelerator Capability. *Research-Technology Management*, *61*(4), 26-34.

Mair, J., & Rathert, N. (2020). Let's Talk about Problems: Advancing Research on Hybrid Organizing, Social Enterprises, and Institutional Context. In M. L. Besharov & B. C. Mitzinneck (Eds.), *Organizational Hybridity: Perspectives, Processes, Promises* (Vol. 69, pp. 189-208). Emerald Publishing Limited.

Mazzei, M. (2017). Understanding Difference: The Importance of 'Place' in the Shaping of Local Social Economies. *VOLUNTAS: International Journal of Voluntary and Nonprofit Organizations*, *28*(6), 2763-2784.

Mcadam, M., & Marlow, S. (2007). Building Futures or Stealing Secrets?:Entrepreneurial Cooperation and Conflict within Business Incubators. *International Small Business Journal*, *25*(4), 361-382.

Merali, Y. (2000). Individual and collective congruence in the knowledge management process. *The Journal of Strategic Information Systems*, *9*(2), 213-234.

Moulaert, F., Martinelli, F., Swyngedouw, E., & Gonzalez, S. (2005). Towards Alternative Model(s) of Local Innovation. *Urban Studies*, *42*(11), 1969-1990.

Nair, P. B. (2022). Embracing Hybridity: A Business Model Innovation for Sustainable Social Enterprises. *International Journal of Business and Society*, *23*(3).

Pache, A.-C., & Chowdhury, I. (2012). Social Entrepreneurs as Institutionally Embedded Entrepreneurs: Toward a New Model of Social Entrepreneurship Education. *Academy of Management Learning & Education*, *11*(3), 494-510.

Pache, A.-C., & Santos, F. (2013). Inside the Hybrid Organization: Selective Coupling as a Response to Competing Institutional Logics. *Academy of Management Journal*, *56*(4), 972-1001.

Pandey, S., Lall, S., Pandey, S. K., & Ahlawat, S. (2017). The Appeal of Social Accelerators: What do Social Entrepreneurs Value? *Journal of Social Entrepreneurship*, *8*(1), 88-109.

Phan, P. H., Siegel, D. S., & Wright, M. (2005). Science parks and incubators: observations, synthesis and future research. *Journal of Business Venturing*, *20*(2), 165-182.

Ponds, R., Van Oort, F., & Frenken, K. (2007). The geographical and institutional proximity of research collaboration*. *Papers in Regional Science*, *86*(3), 423-443.

Presutti, M., Boari, C., & Majocchi, A. (2011). The Importance of Proximity for the Start-Ups' Knowledge Acquisition and Exploitation. *Journal of Small Business Management*, *49*(3), 361-389.

Rawhouser, H., Cummings, M., & Crane, A. (2015). Benefit Corporation Legislation and the Emergence of a Social Hybrid Category. *California Management Review*, *57*(3), 13-35.

Roundy, P. T. (2017). Hybrid organizations and the logics of entrepreneurial ecosystems. *International Entrepreneurship and Management Journal*, *13*(4), 1221-1237.

Rubin, H. J., & Rubin, I. S. (2012). *Qualitative Interviewing: The Art of Hearing Data* (3rd ed.). Thousand Oaks, CA: SAGE Publications, Inc.

Rychen, F., & Zimmermann, J.-B. (2008). Clusters in the Global Knowledge-based Economy: Knowledge Gatekeepers and Temporary Proximity. *Regional Studies*, *42*(6), 767-776.

Sansone, G., Andreotti, P., Colombelli, A., & Landoni, P. (2020). Are social incubators different from other incubators? Evidence from Italy. *Technological Forecasting and Social Change*, *158*, 120132.

Santos, F. M. (2012). A Positive Theory of Social Entrepreneurship. *Journal of Business Ethics*, *111*(3), 335-351.

Schepis, D. (2021). How innovation intermediaries support start-up internationalization: a relational proximity perspective. *Journal of Business & Industrial Marketing*, *36*(11), 2062-2073.

Schutjens, V., & Kruger, M. (2020). The Role of Proximity in Resources Exchanged by Incubatees of Biopartner Center Leiden, the Netherlands. *European Spatial Research and Policy*, *27*(1), 75-104.

Sewell, W. H. (1992). A Theory of Structure: Duality, Agency, and Transformation. *American Journal of Sociology*, *98*(1), 1-29.

Shepherd, D. A., Williams, T. A., & Zhao, E. Y. (2019). A Framework for Exploring the Degree of Hybridity in Entrepreneurship. *Academy of Management Perspectives*, *33*(4), 491-512.

Spradley, J. P. (1980). *Participant Observation*. Long Grove, Illinois: Waveland Press, Inc.

Thomsen, B., Muurlink, O., & Best, T. (2021). Backpack Bootstrapping: Social Entrepreneurship Education Through Experiential Learning. *Journal of Social Entrepreneurship*, *12*(2), 238-264.

Tracey, P., & Phillips, N. (2007). The Distinctive Challenge of Educating Social Entrepreneurs: A Postscript and Rejoinder to the Special Issue on Entrepreneurship Education. *Academy of Management Learning & Education*, *6*(2), 264-271.

Tricarico, L., De Vidovich, L., & Billi, A. (2022). Entrepreneurship, inclusion or co-production? An attempt to assess territorial elements in social innovation literature. *Cities*, *130*, 103986.

Uzzi, B. (1997). Social Structure and Competition in Interfirm Networks: The Paradox of Embeddedness. *Administrative Science Quarterly*, *42*(1), 35-67.

Van Dyck, B., & Van Den Broeck, P. (2013). Social innovation: a territorial process. In *The International Handbook on Social Innovation* (pp. 131-141). Cheltenham, UK: Edward Elgar.

Villani, E., Rasmussen, E., & Grimaldi, R. (2017). How intermediary organizations facilitate university–industry technology transfer: A proximity approach. *Technological Forecasting and Social Change*, *114*, 86-102.

von Schnurbein, G., Potluka, O., & Mayer, A. (2021). Creating social innovation in urban development through collaborative processes. *Innovation: The European Journal of Social Science Research*, 1-17.

Waddock, S., Meszoely, G. M., Waddell, S., & Dentoni, D. (2015). The complexity of wicked problems in large scale change. *Journal of Organizational Change Management*, *28*(6), 993-1012.

Walsh, J. P. (1995). Managerial and Organizational Cognition: Notes from a Trip Down Memory Lane. *Organization Science*, *6*(3), 280-321.

Wei, X., Cang, S., & Hisrich, R. D. (2015). Entrepreneurial Stressors as Predictors of Entrepreneurial Burnout. *Psychological Reports*, *116*(1), 74-88.

Wuyts, S., Colombo, M. G., Dutta, S., & Nooteboom, B. (2005). Empirical tests of optimal cognitive distance. *Journal of Economic Behavior & Organization*, *58*(2), 277-302.

Yang, S., Kher, R., Newbert, S.L. (2020). What signals matter for social startups? It depends: The influence of gender role congruity on social impact accelerator selection decisions. *Journal of Business Venturing*, *35*(2).

Yin, R. (2018). *Case Study Research and Applications: Design and Methods* (6 ed.). Thousand Oaks, CA: SAGE Publications.

Young, D. R., Jung, T., & Aranson, R. (2010). Mission—Market Tensions and Nonprofit Pricing. *The American Review of Public Administration*, *40*(2), 153-169.

Essay Three

Revenue Streams of Social Impact Incubators and Accelerators: The Influence of Program Benefits

Lucca Nietlispach, Georg von Schnurbein

Abstract

In recent years, many initiatives and programs have been developed to strengthen and promote the social economy, but its growth is not meeting the expectations to date. One answer to this lack of development are private support organizations such as social impact incubators and accelerators (SIIAs). However, this new type of organization is not well understood. For example, the determinants of their revenue streams are unknown. In this study, we apply benefits theory of nonprofit finance to SIIAs. We ask how the benefits provided by SIIAs affect the composition of their revenue sources. In line with benefits theory, we hypothesize that SIIAs with programs focused on social benefits are funded by a greater share of donation income and SIIAs with programs focused on economic benefits by greater shares of government income. The data were collected through an international survey. We show that SIIAs with programs that provide social benefits have a greater share of donation income and a lower share of earned income. We also show that SIIAs with programs that provide economic benefits have a greater share of government income and lower share of donation income. This study provides further evidence for the viability of benefits theory. In addition, this study has implications for practitioners. Financial stability is a major challenge for many SIIAs and focusing on the suitable type of funding in relation to their specific benefits can increase their resilience.

Keywords: organizational hybridity, social economy, nonprofit incubator, nonprofit accelerator, social impact incubator, social impact accelerator

Introduction

The social economy is gaining importance as a development approach that is not overly focused on economic goals and profit maximization (Sonnino & Griggs-Trevarthen, 2013). Aside from a small percentage of private and third sector organizations, social enterprises, as hybrids located between the two sectors, are central actors in the social economy. Due to the various challenges that social enterprises face in scaling and growing, organizations have emerged that support them in this endeavor. A prominent type of these support organizations are social impact incubators and accelerators (SIIAs). Incubators and accelerators are a well-researched phenomenon in the business context (Hackett & Dilts, 2004). However, SIIAs are a relatively new type of organization at the crossroads of for-profit and nonprofit organizations (NPOs) that has not been well studied (Sansone et al., 2020). Nevertheless, recent years have shown an increase in research that is specifically focused on SIIAs. SIIAs are a type of intermediary in innovation ecosystems (Ho & Yoon, 2022). They provide different services, such as coworking spaces and consulting (Pandey et al., 2017). In addition, they offer structured innovation programs to cohorts of organizations (Lall et al., 2020). SIIAs must consider social and economic aspects in their strategy and operations, which creates challenges for their management. In particular, generating adequate funding is one of the major obstacles to resilience (Nicolopoulou et al., 2017). SIIAs are often NPOs funded by donation income but can also be formed as a for-profit relying on other types of revenue such as earned or government income. Hence, we consider SIIAs as hybrid organizations with different funding sources at hand.

Given the diversity of SIIAs and the social nature of their purpose, we apply benefits theory of nonprofit finance. It provides nuanced insight into the determinants of funding sources, indicating that the benefits an organization provides determine its funding sources (Young, 2017). There is considerable empirical support for this theory (Aschari-Lincoln & Jäger, 2016; Fischer et al., 2011; Liu & Kim, 2021; Stühlinger & Hersberger-Langloh, 2021; Wilsker & Young, 2010). However, more research is needed that applies this theory to a variety of fields. Thus, we investigate its suitability in the context of organizational hybridity and SIIAs. We ask the following research question:

How do the benefits provided by social impact incubators and accelerators affect the composition of their revenue sources?

We aim to answer this research question by collecting survey data on SIIAs. In contrast to previous studies on SIIAs, which focus on individual countries or regions (Barbero et al., 2014; Hirschmann et al., 2021; Sansone et al., 2020), we conduct a global survey mirroring the global existence of SIIAs. The social media platform LinkedIn served as a primary source for the identification of relevant organizations. This article is one of the first to investigate the funding sources of SIIAs (Valero et al., 2021). The study includes organizations from various institutional contexts. Responses were received from a total of 34 countries on the African, Asian, Australian, European, South and North American continents (Table 19, appendix).

This article is structured as follows: it begins with a review of the literature on SIIAs, organizational hybridity, and funding and benefits theory. Then, the empirical hypotheses are developed based on these theories, and the methods, including the collection and analysis of the data, are explained. The data are analyzed by partial least squares structural equation modeling. Subsequently, the findings are elaborated upon and discussed. Finally, conclusions for research and practice are drawn, and the study's limitations are described.

Literature Review

Social Impact Incubators and Accelerators

Incubators and accelerators are intermediaries in the complex realm of innovation ecosystems (Howells, 2006). They offer diverse services for nascent organizations. In some form or another, incubator and accelerator services have always been offered to startups. However, they are differentiated from other innovation intermediaries by their educational role and their bundling of services into a program (Fiorentino, 2019). These programs combine workshops, coworking space, consulting and networking services in one offering for cohorts of organizations or individuals on a cyclical basis. The literature on incubators and accelerators in the business context is extensive (for an overview, see Mian et al., 2016 and Crişan et al., 2021). This has led to recommendations for best practices that business incubators can follow (Bergek & Norrman, 2008). However, in recent years, an increasing number of incubators have not operated solely according to business orientations. The objectives of other types of incubators are more varied (Barbero et al., 2014) and not focused exclusively on profitability and financial success (Mahmoud-Jouini et al., 2018). For example, a focus on job creation has been ascribed to publicly sponsored organizations (Hausberg & Korreck, 2020). The organizational mission of nonprofit incubators and accelerators often consists of community development (Liu & Van de Walle, 2023). In addition, universities increasingly sponsor and initiate programs (Cooper et al., 2012). Increased recognition of hybrid incubators and accelerators has resulted from the rise of organizations with several objectives (Aernoudt, 2004; Gao & Hu, 2017; Roundy, 2017). In particular, more research is devoted to organizations that have a social goal and aim to participate in market activities at the same time (Bank et al., 2017; Roberts & Lall, 2018; Valero et al., 2021; Yang, 2020). SIIAs are types of incubators or accelerators operating at the intersection of these two aspects. Increasing doubt regarding the feasibility of technological and market innovation to meet societal challenges facilitated this hybrid approach. Furthermore, the importance of collaboration and networks for the success of social innovation has led scholars to increasingly investigate ecosystems of social innovation (Domanski et al., 2019), to which SIIAs belong.

The literature on SIIAs is in its infancy, with few studies investigating this type of organization. SIIAs' hybrid nature is expressed not only in their structural characteristics but also by their exposure of participants to the processes of economic and social value creation (Roundy, 2017). The services they provide consist of "(1) training, (2) mentoring, (3) networking with partners and customers, (4) networking with like-minded entrepreneurs, (5) direct funding through seed capital, (6) indirect funding through access to investors and (7) building awareness and credibility" (Pandey et al., 2017, p. 95). Studies show a positive effect of SIIAs on the emergence of supported organizations (Kher et al., 2022; Lall et al., 2020). Furthermore, studies analyzing the selection process of program participants in SIIAs (Butz & Mrożewski, 2021; Hirschmann et al., 2021) find that the organizations display great heterogeneity and that many struggle to adapt their practices to include a social mission. Although hybridity is central, it is a major practical challenge for SIIAs. To build the conceptual basis for the rest of the article, the following section reviews the literature on organizational hybridity and connects it to SIIAs.

Organizational Hybridity

Organizations of different sectors, such as the nonprofit or private sector, are generally thought to differ because their members follow distinct principles (Billis, 2010) and governance mechanisms (Seibel, 2015). However, this does not apply to hybrid organizations such as corporate foundations (Gehringer, 2021), social enterprises (Doherty et al., 2014), or SIIAs. Hybridity has been studied in the public, private and third sectors because of its strong influence on organizations (Beaton et al., 2021; De Waele et al., 2015; Powell & Sandholtz, 2012). Due to the varied contexts in which organizational hybridity is studied, its meaning can be ambiguous. Research on hybrid organizations has often been criticized because of this lack of conceptual development of hybridity (Billis, 2010). In this study, we focus on the social and economic aspects of SIIAs. Significant advances have been made to better conceptualize this type of hybridity (Lamy, 2019), which will be discussed in the following section.

The specific constellations of the importance of either social or economic aspects vary between organizations. In other words, organizations have different degrees of hybridity (Shepherd et al., 2019). The relationship between economic and social aspects is often conceptualized as a continuum (Battilana et al., 2017). The economic aspect is on one end of the continuum, and the social aspect is on the other (Figure 13). This implies that organizations with a focus on economic aspects have less focus on social aspects, and vice versa. A balanced organization is in the middle. The possible configurations of organizational hybridity vary significantly and are strongly dependent on context. For example, in work integration social enterprises (WISEs), both prioritization of social or economic aspects and balanced prioritization of the two have been observed (Ramus et al., 2016; Woodside, 2018).

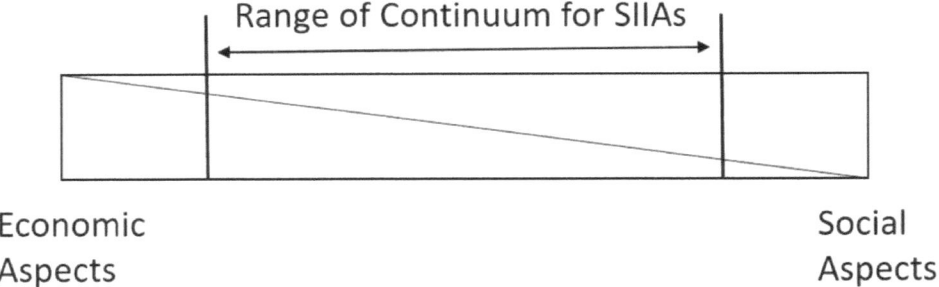

Figure 13: Continuum of social and economic hybridity (own illustration)

Hybridity is present in multiple organizational aspects. These different aspects exhibit different degrees of hybridity (Fu, 2023). Overall, identity (Fauchart & Gruber, 2011; Wry & York, 2017) and attention to goals (Hagedoorn et al., 2022; Yin & Chen, 2019) have been shown to be particularly influential in shaping organizations. Hence, we focus on these two areas to assess SIIAs' overall hybridity.

Organizational identity is defined as "the set of beliefs about what is most core, enduring, and distinctive about an organization" (Voss et al., 2006, p. 741). Numerous studies have assessed organizational identity in hybrid organizations characterized by a social and economic mission. The importance of economic utility is assessed on a continuum against social aspects such as normative aspects (Foreman & Whetten, 2002) or artistic excellence (Glynn, 2000). Organizational identity has also been assessed across different types of hybrid organizations. For example, Moss et al. (2011) investigate organizational identity in social ventures. Furthermore, Foreman and Whetten (2002) analyze identities in hybrid cooperatives. To assess organizations regarding how "business-like" they are, they use the concept of utilitarian organizational identity. A stronger utilitarian mission in these organizations is used to assess the degree of economic benefits that members expect from their participation, indicating greater self-interest and the importance of maximizing profits (Foreman & Whetten, 2002).

Attention must be divided constantly among goals in organizations. Hence, this topic has attracted considerable research interest (Ocasio, 1997; Stevens et al., 2015). Particularly for hybrid organizations with dual goals (Yin & Chen, 2019), attention to goals is important. Specifically, scholars have investigated how the social goals of hybrid organizations can be retained (Sarma, 2020) or incorporated with a commercial goal (Kurland & Schneper, 2021).

The consequences of organizational hybridity can be detrimental for SIIAs. Leaders face challenges due to dual-goal management. Setting a clear goal in advance is not always possible (Schröer & Jäger, 2015). Mission drift is also a major concern (Grimes et al., 2019). Scholars have found that organizational hybridity can positively influence performance (Mongelli et al., 2019), but certain barriers need to be overcome to harness these positive effects (Davies et al., 2019; Salavou & Manolopoulos, 2021; Staessens et al., 2019). One such barrier is targeting and obtaining funding. The next section will discuss the literature on funding and benefits theory in the context of SIIAs.

Funding and Benefits Theory

Hybrid organizations are often funded from different sources (Ji & Konrath, 2023). The benefits theory of nonprofit finance makes predictions regarding how these organizations are financed. It proposes a relationship between funding sources and the benefits organizations provide. Specifically, the mix of benefits determines the mix of funding. For example, an organization that provides public benefits is more likely to be funded by government sources (Young, 2017). Underlying this theory is the transactional nature of the services that social purpose organizations provide. Building on the understanding of transactions from economics (Coase, 1937; Williamson, 1981), it is argued that the activities of social purpose organizations should be considered in terms of exchanges. Hence, a transaction with a social goal and the benefits that arise from it should be aligned with the nature of the funding source. Earned, donation and government income are investigated in more detail in the remainder of this section.

The theory links the generation of private benefits to higher shares of earned income in organizations. Earned income can consist of the sale of products and services, membership fees or event revenues. When an organization intends to participate in market activity, it should take care to assess its competitive advantage beforehand. Administrative capacity, expertise and the potential danger of mission drift should not be neglected either (Young, 2017). Profit generation is not prohibited, but nonprofit organizations are subject to the nondistribution of profit constraint (Scarlata & Alemany, 2010). Accordingly, SIIAs incorporated as nonprofit organizations are allowed to profit from earned income, but they are not allowed to distribute earnings. Hence, profit may exclusively be used to advance the social mission of the organization.

Some benefits of goods and services provided by organizations are shared collectively by a specific group (Young, 2017). These group goods are most often financed by philanthropic funds. Either institutions or individuals can provide these contributions. Donations from foundations and corporations make up a large part of institutional giving (Young, 2017). Overall, donations from individuals make up the most significant share of donation income in the US (Young, 2017). Contributions can also be made as in-kind donations. In this case, their suitability depends on the type of beneficiary activity. In the context of SIIAs and their need for office space, in-kind donations can be appropriate. Nevertheless, the importance of human resources limits the usefulness of in-kind donations as an income source.

Finally, governments are expected to fund goods and services that accrue to the public. Financial support can be provided at many different levels. For example, many SIIAs might be supported by foreign governments. The government can also have financial influence through tax policies and tax exemptions (Young, 2017). In addition, the types of government contribution differ, and governments provide both grants and contracts to SIIAs. Contracts can be recurring and long-term and thus more attractive for SIIAs. Recent research shows that government income is beneficial for the financial health of nonprofit organizations (Thornton & Lecy, 2023). A variety of previous studies have assessed the applicability of benefits theory (Aschari-Lincoln & Jäger, 2016; Wilsker & Young, 2010). Fischer et al. (2011) produce confirming evidence, finding that public services are offered by nonprofits that have the lowest share of earned income. Conversely, the share of earned income is highest for nonprofits that offer private services. Aschari-Lincoln and Jäger (2016) find support for the relationships between private beneficiaries and earned income and between public beneficiaries and donation income. Their results are in line with benefits theory. Furthermore, Liu and Kim (2021) investigate arts and cultural nonprofits. They find supporting evidence that benefit-based revenue has a positive effect on financial health. Wilsker and Young (2010) analyze a sample of Jewish community centers and find that organizations that provide services of a more private nature are associated with higher earned income and that public services are linked to higher donation income.

These findings indicate that the theory is generally supported by empirical evidence; it is also normative and prescribes how founders and leaders of organizations should target funding sources. Apt targeting of funding sources via benefits theory allows organizations to optimally exploit the maximum amount of funding. However, knowledge is lacking about the funding mix of SIIAs. This study addresses this gap in the literature.

Hypotheses Development

The hybridity of SIIAs is exhibited not only in their own identity and attention to goals but also in those of their program participants. Asking respondents to judge organizational identity and attention to the goals of program participants provides a more accurate assessment of the benefits of SIIAs. Hence, we ask SIIAs to assess not their own hybridity but rather that of the program participants that they support. We expect that this greatly reduces social desirability bias.

To assess hybridity and the social and economic orientations of program participants, we assess utilitarian organizational identity and attention to social goals. In order to relate to the literature of organizational hybridity, we use the term economic rather than utilitarian identity. We hypothesize that a focus on economic organizational identity affects the latter because these two constructs vary in nature. Organizational identity is considered enduring. For instance, beliefs are central to identity and not easily changed (Whetten & Mackey, 2002). A specific example of how organizational identity is measured further indicates its enduring nature: staff expertise is a determinant of economic organizational identity (Foreman & Whetten, 2002). Staff expertise is largely formed from previous professional experience and the background of founders or employees. Similarly, the economic value of products and services as a determinant of organizational identity is often established in formal organizational structures such as mission statements. Thus, organizational identity can be considered more enduring than other aspects of the organization, such as attention to social goals. Attention to social goals can shift more easily. Organizations can adapt their goals and change their strategy based on their environment (Kirtley & O'Mahony, 2023; Ocasio, 1997). Many environmental aspects are dependent on the degree to which economic organizational identity is formed over time. Hence, attention to social goals is expected to be influenced by a more enduring economic organizational identity (Figure 14).

The continuum approach of hybridity proposes a conflicting relationship between social and economic aspects in organizations. In line with this approach, we hypothesize that SIIAs focusing on program participants with a stronger economic organizational identity attend less to the social goals of program participants:

H1: SIIAs' greater focus on program participants' economic identity negatively influences their focus on program participants' attention to social goals.

In addition to the relationship between the social and economic aspects of hybridity, we hypothesize that economic organizational identity and attention to the social goals of SIIAs' program participants affect the funding mix. We take benefits theory of nonprofit finance as the theoretical foundation for our hypothesis development. An SIIA's focus on economically oriented programs is an indication of the private nature of its benefits. Private benefits are associated with higher shares of earned income. Economically oriented program participants have greater capacity to generate earned income themselves; thus, SIIAs are more likely to be able to generate income from more financially capable organizations. However, an SIIA's focus on economically oriented program participants can also be an indication of greater emphasis on economic development. Due to the public benefits of economic development, the share of government funding is also expected to be greater for SIIAs with a focus on economically oriented participants. For example, previous research has shown that specific policies support incubators and accelerators to promote economic development (Mian et al., 2016). Conversely, we expect a lower share of donation income for SIIAs with a focus on economically oriented program participants. We formulate the following hypotheses in regard to SIIAs with a greater focus on program participants' economic organizational identity:

H2a: A greater focus of SIIAs on program participants' economic organizational identity leads to a greater share of earned income.
H2b: A greater focus of SIIAs on program participants' economic organizational identity leads to a greater share of government income.
H2c: A greater focus of SIIAs on program participants' economic organizational identity leads to a lower share of donation income.

An SIIA's focus on socially oriented program participants suggests that its benefits are of a group nature. Group benefits are associated with higher shares of donation income. Nonprofit organizations often support specific groups in need, such as elderly people (Jing et al., 2021). In addition to higher shares of donation income, we also expect higher shares of government income. Governments have repeatedly stepped in to fund vulnerable groups (Clifford et al., 2013; Wiesel & Liu, 2021). Furthermore, group benefits are associated with lower shares of earned income because SIIAs are not able to charge beneficiaries directly (Young, 2017). Accordingly, we formulate the following hypotheses in regard to a greater focus of SIIAs on program participants' attention to social goals:

H3a: A greater focus of SIIAs on program participants' attention to social goals leads to a lower share of earned income.
H3b: A greater focus of SIIAs on program participants' attention to social goals leads to a greater share of government income.
H3c: A greater focus of SIIAs on program participants' attention to social goals leads to a greater share of donation income.

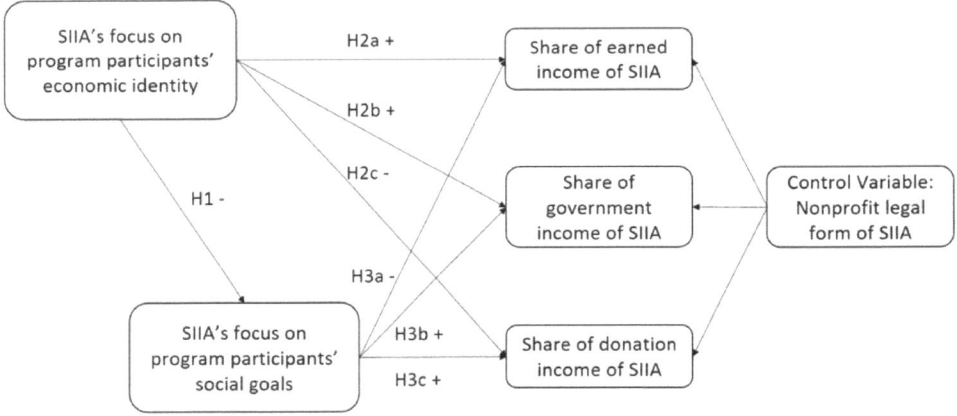

Figure 14: Empirical model

Methodology

Sample and Data Collection

We gathered a unique dataset. Relevant organizations were identified through three sources. First, the majority of organizations were identified through the social media platform LinkedIn. We used machine learning to identify the email addresses of organizations on LinkedIn. This process took place between the 12th and 21st of August 2023. On LinkedIn, a variety of search terms were used to identify SIIAs (Table 9).

"Incubator" search terms	"Accelerator" search terms
Nonprofit incubator	Nonprofit accelerator
Non-profit incubator	Non-profit accelerator
Non profit incubator	Non profit accelerator
Social incubator	Social accelerator
Social impact incubator	Social impact accelerator
Impact incubator	Impact accelerator
Social innovation incubator	Social innovation accelerator
Social venture incubator	Social venture accelerator
Social enterprise incubator	Social enterprise accelerator

Table 9: LinkedIn search terms

Second, a list of website addresses of 309 organizations studied in a landscape report of social enterprise incubators in 2020 (Sours et al., 2020) served as a source. The list was obtained by email through personal contact with the organization that published the report. The Global Accelerator Learning Initiative (GALI) directory served as the third source. It is assembled by the Aspen Network of Development Entrepreneurs (ANDE) and Emory University. The directory contains a list of accelerators, including website addresses (GALI, 2023). It collects data from several hundred accelerators that are freely available for download (GALI, 2023). Both the landscape report and the GALI directory were scraped between the 21st and 23rd of August 2023. In total, 2232 organizations with at least one email address were identified through machine learning algorithms (Table 10). A standardized electronic questionnaire was developed on Qualtrics. It contained general questions regarding, for example, the legal form or focus area of programs and organizational hybridity and funding sources. The questionnaire was sent by email to one email address per organization.

Source	Identified organizations	Identified websites	Identified email addresses
LinkedIn	3834	3441	1845
Report	309	309	197
GALI	403	403	225
Combined (no duplicates)	4494	4101	2232

Table 10: Web scraping results

A total of 127 survey responses were received between August 25th and October 19th, 2023. Twenty-two respondents indicated that they did not participate in an incubator or accelerator program and were removed from the sample.[1] Furthermore, 14 data entries had to be removed due to unreasonable or missing data.[2] In addition, two entries had to be deleted because they were duplicates that were submitted from the same IP address.[3] The final sample comprised 89 responding organizations.

The largest number of respondents in the sample is from North America. Thirty-four responses were received from IP addresses in the US, and six were received from IP addresses in Canada. Six responses were received from India, four from Switzerland and three from Germany. The remaining responses were received from countries on the continents of Europe, Africa, Asia, Australia and South America (Table 19, appendix). SIIAs are often rather young organizations, with an average age of 9.4 years. Fifty respondent organizations employ five or fewer employees. One organization is completely volunteer-led with zero paid staff. Most often, SIIAs conduct one incubator or accelerator program per year. The maximum number of programs conducted by an organization is ten (Table 11). Approximately two-thirds of the respondents indicated that their organization has a specific thematic focus in their program. ICT, education, agriculture and food, health and the environment are some of the most prominent focus areas. Thirty-seven respondents indicated that their organization provides direct funding to program participants. Seventy organizations operate with a nonprofit legal form. Fourteen SIIAs are incorporated with a for-profit legal form, and the remaining five organizations operate through other hybrid legal forms (Table 12). Nineteen of the nonprofit organizations are not tax exempt. The survey measured respondents' funding sources in the following four categories: government, earned, donation and investment income. In terms of revenue diversification, 75% of organizations have more than one of the four categories of revenue sources. Revenue diversification was also measured with the Herfindahl–Hirschman index (HHI) (Chang & Tuckman, 1994), with government, earned, donation and investment income as separate income categories. The normalized HHI takes values between zero and one and was calculated as proposed by Mayer et al. (2014). In this study, the mean value is 0.38, which indicates a relatively high level of revenue diversification in SIIAs.

Variable	Minimum	Median	Mean	SD	Maximum
Organization's age (in years)	0.5	7.0	9.4	9.2	62.0
Employees (in FTE)	0.0	5.0	467.4	4294.8	40528.0
Volunteers (in FTE)	0.0	4.0	46.6	317.5	3000.0
Number of incubator programs	0.0	1.0	1.4	1.5	6.0
Number of accelerator programs	0.0	1.0	1.4	1.5	10.0
Share of government income (in %)	0.0	14.1	32.4	36.3	100.0
Share of earned income (in %)	0.0	9.1	20.1	28.4	100.0
Share of donation income (in %)	0.0	27.5	38.2	37.7	100.0
Share of investment income (in %)	0.0	14.7	29.3	34.3	100.0
HHI index (normalized)	0.00	0.43	0.39	0.31	0.93

Table 11: Descriptive statistics of variables (N=89)

Legal form	Number of organizations
Nonprofit (e.g., foundation, cooperative, association)	70
For-profit (e.g., business corporation, limited liability company)	14
Other (hybrid legal forms)	5

Table 12: Legal forms of organizations

Data Analysis

The data were analyzed using partial least squares structural equation modeling (PLS-SEM). The share of published articles applying PLS-SEM has increased significantly in the last decade (Hair et al., 2019). The method is regularly applied in a wide range of disciplines (Sarstedt et al., 2020), including nonprofit (Hengevoss, 2023) and social entrepreneurship (Kannampuzha & Hockerts, 2019) research. The method emphasizes the ability to make predictions from data. This makes it suitable for developing managerial implications. Furthermore, it does not impose distributional assumptions on the data (Sarstedt et al., 2016). PLS-SEM has been shown to have greater statistical power than other methods (Hair et al., 2019). Partial regression relationships are computed separately using ordinary least squares regressions (Hair et al., 2017; Reinartz et al., 2009). The model was estimated in RStudio using the package SEMinR. A total of 10,000 bootstrap samples were used for all the model estimations as recommended by Streukens and Leroi-Werelds (2016).

Measurement Model Assessment

The independent variables in this study are SIIA's focus on program participants' economic organizational identity and SIIA's focus on program participants' attention to social goals. They are latent constructs with measurement items that were adopted from previous studies. Both latent variables are reflectively measured.

To determine the economic organizational identity of SIIA program participants, the operationalization of Foreman and Whetten (2002) was applied. Higher economic identity implies greater importance of the economic value and prices of products and services, as well as professionalization and staff expertise (Stevens et al., 2015). In the questionnaire, we measured SIIA leaders' perception of the organizational identity of program participants (ECID). The indicators were measured with a 7-point Likert scale. The model was originally estimated with five, as well as four, indicator items for economic organizational identity (see appendix). However, convergent validity, indicated by the average variance extracted (AVE), was below the threshold of 0.5 (5-ECID AVE: 0.486/4-ECID AVE: 0.486). Hence, two items were dropped, and the model was estimated with three indicator items and a satisfactory AVE value (3-ECID AVE: 0.504). The loadings of two of the three indicators in the model with the three indicators were slightly below 0.708. Indicators above 0.6 are acceptable in exploratory research (Hair et al., 2022). Hence, the model was estimated with three indicators due to the higher AVE value. The internal consistency reliability and composite reliability (CR) values were above the threshold of 0.7 and thus satisfactory (Table 13).

The measure of Aupperle et al. (1985) was employed to measure the construct of attention to social goals. It is based on four categories of responsibilities that firms need to fulfill: economic, legal, ethical and discretionary. The focus is on discretionary social responsibilities, which SI-IAs consider important for their program participants. Discretionary goals are philanthropic in nature and are characterized by a social nature. For example, survey respondents were asked about the importance of addressing social issues and creating value for society. Stevens et al. (2015) applied this scale to develop a measurement construct for the social and economic missions of social enterprises. This measure has been used in a variety of studies (Agle et al., 1999; Angelidis & Ibrahim, 2004; Ibrahim & Angelidis, 1995; Ibrahim et al., 2000; Ibrahim et al., 2008; Stevens et al., 2015). Questionnaire respondents were asked to allocate 10 points among the four areas. This ipsative scale has advantages compared to Likert scales. In Likert-type questions, respondents are likely to score both social and economic goals highly. On the ipsative scale, they have to choose between the two or score both equally low. Thus, socially desirable answers are reduced (Aupperle et al., 1985; Stevens et al., 2015). The original instrument contains 20 sets of four items. All the items are employed to measure the same information (Aupperle et al., 1985). To avoid increasing the survey response time and maximize the number of responses, four sets of four items were used. This approach of reducing the number of items is in line with that of other scholars (Agle et al., 1999; Stevens et al., 2015).

A model with all four indicators for the construct attention to social goals (SOCG) was evaluated first. The loading of one indicator were below the threshold of 0.708. We compared reliability and validity measures against a model in which the weakest indicator was removed. The model with only three indicators per construct showed improved indicator reliability. The AVE improved (4-SOCG AVE: 0.560 vs. 3-SOCG AVE: 0.639). The internal consistency reliability of the SOCG indicated by the composite reliability (CR) was relatively unchanged (4-SOCG CR: 0.835/3-SOCG CR: 0.841).

To assess discriminant validity, heterotrait-monotrait ratio (HTMT) values were inspected (Table 14). Henseler et al. (2015) propose a conservative threshold for the HTMT value of 0.85 and a threshold of 0.9 for conceptually similar constructs. The HTMT value regarding ECID and SOCG was 0.414. In addition, we tested the bootstrap confidence interval for HTMT at a 5% upper boundary in line with Aguirre-Urreta and Rönkkö (2017). The upper boundary of the 90% two-sided bootstrap confidence interval was 0.620. It was thus below the threshold of 0.85. We concluded that discriminant validity existed.

The latent construct of attention to social goals was also a dependent variable. The three other dependent variables were the shares of funding sources. In the survey, all the funding sources were categorized into four major categories: government, earned[4], donation[5] and investment income.[67] Our model included the shares of earned, donation and government income. The share of a funding source was calculated as a percentage of total income.[8] To calculate the model, two latent variables were estimated with one indicator variable with a 1.0 indicator loading each.

Construct		Items	Loading	α	CR (rhoᴄ)	AVE	Reliability coefficient (rhoₐ)
SIIA's focus on program participants' economic		Please indicate your perception of the importance that program participants place on each of the following aspects:		0.748	0.752	0.504	0.756
identity	ECID1	Economic value of products and services	0.691				
	ECID2	Price of products and services	0.771				
	ECID3	Professionalism/expertise of staff	0.664				
SIIA's focus on program participants' social		It is important that program participants:		0.839	0.841	0.639	0.847
	SOCG1	have the possibility to participate in activities that address social issues	0.736				
cial goals	SOCG2	examine regularly new opportunities and programs which can result in an increase in value for society	0.879				
	SOCG3	attend to addressing societal problems	0.776				

Table 13: Construct validity

	1	2
ECID		
SOCG	0.414 [CI.900 0.236 0.620]	

Table 14: HTMT values

Structural model assessment

The regressions of the structural model were assessed for collinearity problems through an investigation of the variance inflation factor (VIF) values. The VIF values were 1.119 for the economic organizational identity of program participants, 1.121 for attention to the social goals of program participants and 1.002 for the control variable nonprofit legal form. All the indicators were well below the threshold value of 3 (Hair et al., 2021).

Hypothesis 1 was confirmed (Table 16): A focus of SIIAs on program participants' economic organizational identity had a negative and significant effect on SIIAs' focus on program participants' attention to social goals ($\beta = -0.407$, $t = -3.202$, $p < 0.01$). Furthermore, Hypotheses 2c and 3c were confirmed: A focus of SIIAs on the economic organizational identity of program participants had a negative and significant effect ($\beta = -0.282$, $t = -2.110$, $p < 0.05$), and SIIAs focus on program participants' attention to social goals had a positive and significant effect ($\beta = 0.293$, $t = 2.418$, $p < 0.05$) on the SIIAs' share of donation income (DI). In addition, the effect of SIIAs' focus on program participants' attention to social goals on the SIIAs' share of earned income (EI) was significant and negative ($\beta = -0.372$, $t = -3.358$, $p < 0.01$). Thus, Hypothesis 3a was also supported. In addition, we found supporting evidence for Hypothesis 2b: We found a significant positive effect of a focus of SIIAs on the economic organizational identity of program participants on government income (GI) ($\beta = 0.365$, $t = 2.499$, $p < 0.05$). The effect of SIIAs' focus on economic organizational identity or program participants on the SIIAs' share of earned income was negative and not significant ($\beta = -0.191$, $t = -1.462$, $p > 0.05$). Hence, Hypothesis 2a was not supported. In addition, the effect of attention to program participants' social goals on government income was not significant, and Hypothesis 3b was not supported ($\beta = -0.002$, $t = -0.015$, $p > 0.05$).

Regarding the control variables, a nonprofit legal form had a positive and significant effect on SIIAs' share of donation income ($\beta = 0.196$, $t = 2.380$, $p < 0.05$). Furthermore, the total path from a focus of SIIAs on the economic organizational identity of program participants on the share of donation income was negative and significant ($\beta = -0.401$, $t = -3.563$, $p > 0.01$) and positive and significant on the share of government income ($\beta = -0.366$, $t = -3.179$, $p > 0.01$).

The R^2 value allowed us to assess the model's explanatory power (Table 15). The adjusted R^2 value accounted for the model complexity. The amount of variance explained by the model was highest for the dependent variable share of the SIIAs' donation income (R^2 adj. = .252). The other three dependent variables reached values of approximately 0.1 to 0.15. Thus, the model was able to explain less of the amount of variance in the share of earned income (R^2 adj. = .098) and government income (R^2 adj. = .103) of the SIIA. Furthermore, the model explained approximately 16% of program participants' attention to social goals (R^2 adj. = 0.158). Thus, the model had adequate explanatory power (Hair et al., 2019).

	EI	DI	GI	SOCG
R²	0.127	0.277	0.134	0.167
R² adj.	0.096	0.252	0.103	0.158

Table 15: Model's explanatory power

Effects	β	*t* value	BC 95% Bootstrap CI		Remark
			2.5%	**97.5%**	
H1. ECID → SOCG	-0.407	-3.202**	-0.640	-0.154	Supported
H2a. ECID → EI	-0.191	-1.462	-0.442	0.067	Not supported
H2b. ECID → GI	0.365	2.499*	0.077	0.651	Supported
H2c. ECID → DI	-0.282	-2.110*	-0.549	-0.030	Supported
H3a. SOCG → EI	-0.372	-3.358**	-0.591	-0.158	Supported
H3b. SOCG → GI	-0.002	-0.015	-0.278	0.290	Not supported
H3c. SOCG → DI	0.293	2.418*	0.041	0.511	Supported
Control variables					
Nonprofit legal form → EI	-0.085	-0.707	-0.314	0.150	
Nonprofit legal form → GI	0.018	0.170	-0.197	0.222	
Nonprofit legal form → DI	0.196	2.380*	0.027	0.353	
Total Paths					
ECID → EI	-0.039	-0.337	-0.267	0.191	
ECID → GI	0.366	3.179**	0.129	0.585	
ECID → DI	-0.401	-3.563**	-0.617	-0.176	

Note(s): *p < 0.05 and **p < 0.01

Table 16: Hypothesis testing and results estimation

Furthermore, the impact of the sample size was assessed. A general rule of thumb is to assess the minimum sample size requirement in relation to the most complex model relationship (Peng & Lai, 2012). Inner and outer model links to any latent variable multiplied by 10 should not exceed the sample size. However, this rule of thumb does not take into account effect sizes. In response, Kock and Hadaya (2018) proposed the inverse square root method. Assuming that statistical power is greater than 0.8 and the significance level is 0.05, the minimum sample size required is 78. Hence, the sample size requirements are met.

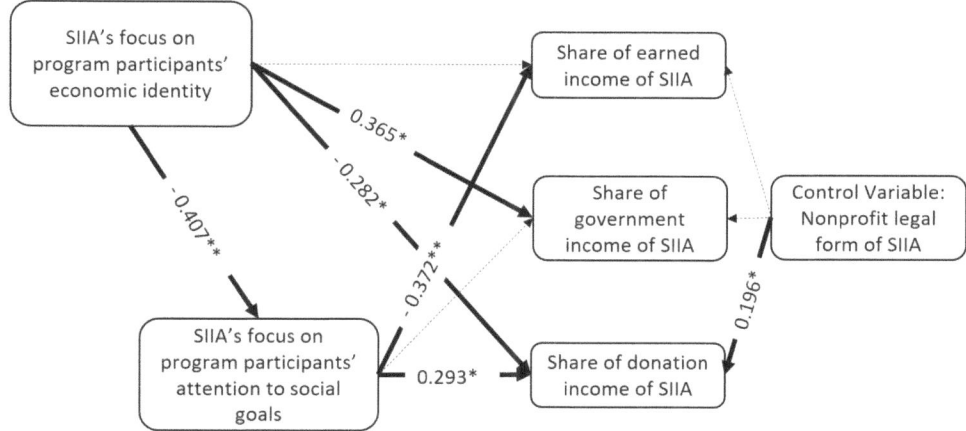

Figure 15: Path model with significant correlations

Discussion

This paper investigated the funding structure and organizational hybridity in SIIAs. We applied benefits theory to determine the effect of the type of benefits on funding sources. Because the benefits of SIIAs depend on the nature of the beneficiaries, such as program participants, we investigated and differentiated the types of SIIAs' program participants. We focused specifically on economic organizational identity and attention to social goals as central aspects of their hybridity. The continuum approach of organizational hybridity conceptualizes these social and economic aspects to be opposing poles on a spectrum. Hypotheses were elaborated based on both benefits theory of nonprofit finance and the continuum approach of organizational hybridity.

The results confirm the continuum approach of organizational hybridity in the context of SIIAs. A focus of SIIAs on the economic identity of program participants leads to less focus on the social goals of program participants. Although some scholars identify benefits of a combination of social and economic aspects (Ashforth & Reingen, 2014; Battilana & Dorado, 2010), this study shows that organizations struggle to maintain high levels of focus on both aspects. The statistical strength of the negative effect of an economic organizational identity on attention to social goals speaks to the extent of this challenge for participants in SIIA programs (Figure 15). This is in line with previous literature indicating tensions between social and economic orientations (Siwale et al., 2021; Woodside, 2018).

Furthermore, we find evidence in line with benefits theory. The evidence is particularly strong in regard to the group benefits of SIIAs. A focus of SIIAs on the social goals of program participants leads to higher shares of donation income and lower shares of earned income. This effect on a lower share of earned income is statistically strong. The possible reason for this is that SIIAs are prevented from earning revenue from their program participants and related stakeholders because of their low financial capacities. Thus, SIIAs are more reliant on donation income. Conversely, we also expected that a focus of SIIAs on the economic organizational identity of program participants would lead to an increase in the share of SIIAs' earned income. The reasoning is that economically oriented program participants earn more revenue themselves. Thus, they would be able to pay for the SIIAs' services. However, the empirical results do not confirm this relationship. SIIAs' ability to generate earned income seems to not be connected to economically oriented program participants. Due to the positive effect of a focus on economically oriented program participants on the share of government income, we assume that government income crowds out earned income. Government support for business incubators and accelerators as a policy to promote economic development has already been observed (Clausen & Rasmussen, 2011; Mian et al., 2016). This study shows that governments also fund SIIAs that lean toward the private sector in their orientation. This is also in line with previous studies that have found social enterprises to clearly prioritize economic over social missions to increase legitimacy in the eyes of the government (Alsaid & Ambilichu, 2021). Conversely, a focus on attention to social goals is not associated with higher levels of government income. The findings also indicate that SIIAs with a focus on economically oriented program participants acquire less donation income.

Scholars support the notion of a blurring of sectors (Billis, 2010). Despite criticism of the blurring hypothesis (Child et al., 2016), there are indications that organizations of one particular legal form are becoming less prototypical (Nunes et al., 2023). Thus, we also controlled for the legal form of SIIAs in our analysis to consider the effect of sector affiliation on funding sources. The results indicate that a nonprofit legal form is a significant predictor of higher shares of donation income. This is partly explained by the legal difficulties for for-profit organizations in receiving donation income. Beyond this relationship, this study shows that the legal form of SIIAs is not a good indicator of organizations' identity, goals, and ultimately funding. For example, for-profit organizations might have a social mission and not be able to earn a large amount of earned income. Furthermore, incubators and accelerators incorporated as nonprofit organizations might exclusively focus their support services on highly economically oriented ventures (Vanderstraeten & Matthyssens, 2012).

In conclusion, SIIAs' program benefits provide a better indicator of funding structure than their legal forms. However, due to the institutional complexity of the environment in which SIIAs operate, we expect that a variety of other factors codetermine funding sources. Unsurprisingly, we find that R^2 values do not exceed 30%. The funding mix is expected to be strongly influenced by other factors (Young et al., 2010), such as stakeholder interests (Berrett & Holliday, 2018). Furthermore, there are specific influencing factors depending on the context of the incubator or accelerator (Ji & Konrath, 2023). However, the results of this study are substantial and indicate a significant effect of SIIAs' benefits on funding structure (Hair et al., 2011).

Conclusion

This study has implications for benefits theory. Most prominently, we contribute to the empirical evidence of benefits theory in the context of SIIAs, despite their high level of institutional complexity. Thus, the results speak to the strength and wide applicability of the theory. We identify differences in the nature of SIIAs' benefits that have a significant effect on the type of funding source. This study focused particularly on programs as a central offering of SIIAs.

SIIAs provide a mix of private, group and public benefits. Their indirect and direct benefits can be differentiated. On the one hand, SIIAs impact program participants directly through their services and promote their organizational development. On the other hand, SIIAs can have indirect benefits for society. When program participants develop into successful organizations, they impact their own clients and beneficiaries. By assuming similar program participant numbers to those in the study by Lall et al. (2020) on impact-oriented ventures, we estimate that the scope of programs in this study affects a total of approximately 3000 program participants per year [9]. Thus, SIIAs can have considerable impact beyond the program level. Economically oriented SIIAs provide economic value for society, for example, in terms of job creation (Sentana et al., 2018). Socially oriented SIIAs broadly promote the social economy as well as specific fields such as education or health, although to what degree they are able to do so is not conclusively established in this study.

There are also implications for the literature on organizational hybridity. This study shows that SIIAs support a wide range of program participants with different orientations. Economic organizational identity and attention to social goals have been shown to vary from low to high. This study provides evidence in support of the continuum approach to organizational hybridity due to the negative effect of economic organizational identity on attention to social goals.

In terms of practical implications, the results strongly suggest that SIIAs with socially oriented program participants should target donation income. Generating earned income will be difficult for these SIIAs. In contrast, SIIAs that benefit economically oriented program participants are best served by targeting the government as a funder. The implications regarding the relationship between the economic orientation of program participants and earned income are less clear because of our mixed results. When the goal of SIIAs is financial stability, adding earned income to the funding mix when possible is reasonable (von Schnurbein & Fritz, 2017). Furthermore, SIIAs are often small organizations, with 50% having five or fewer employees and four or fewer volunteers. Thus, SIIAs should be aware of additional demands when diversifying their funding mix. Practitioners should also be aware of the limitations that legal forms impose on SIIAs' funding possibilities. For example, managers should take note of the difficulties for for-profit entities in receiving donation income. However, in terms of the targeted program participants, the legal form is not a decisive factor. There is ample room to maneuver with regard to one specific legal form. Nonprofit SIIAs can target economically oriented participants with their services, for example, when funded by corporate foundations. For-profit SIIAs can be strongly guided by social goals and implement profit redistribution constraints. Furthermore, SIIA managers should be aware of their multifaceted role as educators. Education incubators and accelerators serve to introduce participants to social and economic value creation (Roundy, 2017). Explicit knowledge of where program participants lie on the continuum of hybridity allows SIIAs to target their services more effectively.

This study has certain limitations. Hypotheses have been developed by building on the continuum approach to organizational hybridity. However, degrees of organizational hybridity can manifest in organizations beyond a simple continuum. For example, the logic multiplicity framework (Besharov & Smith, 2014) and a corresponding quantitative measurement scale (Fu, 2023) have been developed. This framework and others (Shepherd et al., 2019) provide a more nuanced approach to organizational hybridity. They assess hybridity not in one dimension, as in the continuum approach, but in two dimensions. For example, the logic multiplicity framework proposes that organizations display different degrees of hybridity in the compatibility and centrality of logics (Besharov & Smith, 2014). These frameworks remain to be tested with empirical data.

Increasing efforts toward better social performance measurement could contribute significantly to SIIAs' attractiveness for funders by showing achieved social impact. In particular, donation income could increase, and the attractiveness of SIIAs for government funders could be positively influenced. However, multiple problems with social performance measurement need to be overcome. First, there is generally limited understanding of how hybrid organizations can measure performance (Ahearn & Mai, 2023). Second, as this study shows, SIIAs have specific challenges that need to be considered and a one-size-fits-all approach is unsuitable.

[1] These organizations mostly consisted of other types of innovation intermediaries and support organizations such as coworking spaces.

[2] In many of these cases, the numbers indicating the funding sources were either missing or unreasonably low.

[3] For both responses, the email addresses were provided. The respondents indicated that they had submitted the response twice by accident. After clarifying which of the two entries to delete with both respondents, two further answers were removed.

[4] In the questionnaire, we further differentiated earned income among the sale of products and services, membership fees and event revenues.

[5] In the questionnaire, we further differentiated donation income among private, foundation, corporate and in-kind donations.

[6] In 7 cases, other funding sources were indicated. In 4 of these cases, it was clear whether they relied on earned income or donation income. In 3 cases, respondents were contacted by email and indicated whether the other funding source should be categorized as earned or donation income.

[7] Six for-profit organizations indicated that they received donation income. These organizations were further investigated because of the legal limitation in some countries on for-profit entities' receipt of donation income. These instances could be clarified by email in four cases and a visit to the website in another case. In one case, reasonableness could not be confirmed. Due to the legality of the practice in many countries, this case was not excluded. Hence, all six were deemed reasonable.

[8] Respondents were first asked to provide information regarding the distribution of their funding sources in USD. In case they did not make any entries, they were further asked to provide respective percentages of the funding sources from total funding. Fifteen respondents only provided percentages. All the funding sources were converted to percentages for the model estimation.

[9] Lall et al. (2020) study 77 impact-oriented accelerator programs with 904 participants. By multiplying the average number of participants per program with the total number of programs offered by SIIAs in this study, we estimate that the programs of the organizations in this study affect a total of 2,993 (255*(904/77)) participants.

Appendix

Indicator	Survey Items	Factor loading	Mean	SD
	Based on the relative importance and application to program participants, please allocate up to, but not more than, 10 points to each set of four statements.			
SOCG 1	It is important that program participants: (legal) fulfill legal requirements (econ) maximize long-term return on investment (discr) have the possibility to participate in activities that address social issues (ethic) do not make promises which are not intended to be fulfilled when securing new opportunities	0.736	2.920	1.800
SOCG 2	It is important that program participants: (econ) allocate resources on their ability to improve long-term profitability (legal) comply with new laws (discr) examine regularly new opportunities and programs which can result in an increase in value for society (ethic) recognize and respect new or evolving ethical/moral norms adopted by society	0.879	2.890	1.510
	Program participants are successful when: (econ) they are consistently profitable (legal) they fulfill their legal obligations (ethic) they fulfill their ethical and moral responsibilities (discr) they fulfill their philanthropic and charitable responsibilities			
SOCG 3	It is important that program participants attend to: (econ) being as profitable as possible (discr) addressing societal problems (legal) abiding by laws and regulations (ethic) moral and ethical behavior	0.776	3.180	1.840

Table 17: Survey items for attention to goals

Indicator	Survey Item Organizational Identity	Factor loading	Mean	SD
	Please indicate your perception of the importance that program participants place on each of the following aspects:			
ECID1	Economic value of products and services (1) Customer service (2)	0.691	5.490	1.090
ECID2	Price of products and services (3)	0.771	5.210	1.030
ECID3	Professionalism/expertise of staff (4) Quality of products or services (5)	0.664	5.600	1.030

Table 18: Survey items for utilitarian identity

Country	Count
United States of America	34
India	6
Canada	6
Switzerland	4
Germany	3
Uganda	2
United Kingdom of Great Britain and Northern Ireland	2
Democratic Republic of the Congo	2
Australia	2
South Africa	2
Greece	2
Portugal	2
Cyprus	1
Ireland	1
Romania	1
Finland	1
Indonesia	1
Czech Republic	1
Turkey	1
Somalia	1
Nigeria	1
Mexico	1
Austria	1
Norway	1
Hong Kong	1
Cambodia	1
Mongolia	1
Brazil	1
Pakistan	1
Italy	1
Cameroon	1
Kenya	1
Mauritius	1
United Arab Emirates	1

Table 19: Number of respondent IP addresses in respective country

References

Aernoudt, R. (2004). Incubators: Tool for Entrepreneurship? *Small Business Economics*, *23*(2), 127-135.

Agle, B. R., Mitchell, R. K., & Sonnenfeld, J. A. (1999). Who Matters to CEOs? An Investigation of Stakeholder Attributes and Salience, Corporate Performance, and CEO Values. *The Academy of Management Journal*, *42*(5), 507-525.

Aguirre-Urreta, M., & Rönkkö, M. (2017). Statistical Inference with PLSc Using Bootstrap Confidence Intervals. *MIS Quarterly*, *42*.

Ahearn, E.-R., & Mai, C. (2023). The nature of measurement across the hybridised social sector: A systematic review of reviews. *Australian Journal of Public Administration*, *n/a*(n/a).

Alsaid, L., & Ambilichu, C. A. (2021). The influence of institutional pressures on the implementation of a performance measurement system in an Egyptian social enterprise. *Qualitative Research in Accounting and Management*, *18*(1), 53-83.

Angelidis, J., & Ibrahim, N. (2004). An Exploratory Study of the Impact of Degree of Religiousness Upon an Individual's Corporate Social Responsiveness Orientation. *Journal of Business Ethics*, *51*(2), 119-128.

Aschari-Lincoln, J., & Jäger, U. P. (2016). Analysis of Determinants of Revenue Sources for International NGOs:Influence of Beneficiaries and Organizational Characteristics. *Nonprofit and Voluntary Sector Quarterly*, *45*(3), 612-629.

Ashforth, B. E., & Reingen, P. H. (2014). Functions of Dysfunction: Managing the Dynamics of an Organizational Duality in a Natural Food Cooperative. *Administrative Science Quarterly*, *59*(3), 474-516.

Aupperle, K. E., Carroll, A. B., & Hatfield, J. D. (1985). An Empirical Examination of the Relationship between Corporate Social Responsibility and Profitability. *The Academy of Management Journal*, *28*(2), 446-463.

Bank, N., Fichter, K., & Klofsten, M. (2017). Sustainability-profiled incubators and securing the inflow of tenants – The case of Green Garage Berlin. *Journal of Cleaner Production*, *157*, 76-83.

Barbero, J. L., Casillas, J. C., Wright, M., & Ramos Garcia, A. (2014). Do different types of incubators produce different types of innovations? *The Journal of Technology Transfer*, *39*(2), 151-168.

Battilana, J., Besharov, M. L., & Mitzinneck, B. C. (2017). On hybrids and hybrid organizing: A review and roadmap for future research.

Battilana, J., & Dorado, S. (2010). Building Sustainable Hybrid Organizations: The Case of Commercial Microfinance Organizations. *The Academy of Management Journal*, *53*(6), 1419-1440.

Beaton, E., MacIndoe, H., & Wang, T. (2021). Combining Nonprofit Service and Advocacy: Organizational Structures and Hybridity. *Nonprofit and Voluntary Sector Quarterly*, *50*(2), 372-396.

Bergek, A., & Norrman, C. (2008). Incubator best practice: A framework. *Technovation*, *28*(1), 20-28.

Berrett, J. L., & Holliday, B. S. (2018). The Effect of Revenue Diversification on Output Creation in Nonprofit Organizations: A Resource Dependence Perspective. *VOLUNTAS: International Journal of Voluntary and Nonprofit Organizations*, *29*(6), 1190-1201.

Besharov, M. L., & Smith, W. K. (2014). Multiple Institutional Logics in Organizations: Explaining Their Varied Nature and Implications. *Academy of Management Review*, *39*(3), 364-381.

Billis, D. (2010). Towards a theory of hybrid organizations. In D. Billis (Ed.), *Hybrid organizations and the third sector: Challenges for practice, theory and policy* (pp. 46-69). Basingstoke, Hampshire, UK: Palgrave Macmillan.

Butz, H., & Mrożewski, M. J. (2021). The Selection Process and Criteria of Impact Accelerators. An Exploratory Study. *Sustainability*, *13*(12).

Chang, C. F., & Tuckman, H. P. (1994). Revenue diversification among non-profits. *VOLUNTAS: International Journal of Voluntary and Nonprofit Organizations*, *5*(3), 273-290.

Child, C., Witesman, E., & Spencer, R. (2016). The Blurring Hypothesis Reconsidered: How Sector Still Matters to Practitioners. *VOLUNTAS: International Journal of Voluntary and Nonprofit Organizations*, *27*(4), 1831-1852.

Clausen, T., & Rasmussen, E. (2011). Open innovation policy through intermediaries: the industry incubator programme in Norway. *Technology Analysis & Strategic Management*, *23*(1), 75-85.

Clifford, D., Geyne-Rahme, F., & Mohan, J. (2013). Variations between Organisations and Localities in Government Funding of Third-sector Activity: Evidence from the National Survey of Third-sector Organisations in England. *Urban Studies*, *50*(5), 959-976.

Coase, R. H. (1937). The Nature of the Firm. *Economica*, *4*(16), 386-405.

Cooper, C. E., Hamel, S. A., & Connaughton, S. L. (2012). Motivations and obstacles to networking in a university business incubator. *The Journal of Technology Transfer*, *37*(4), 433-453.

Crişan, E. L., Salanţă, I. I., Beleiu, I. N., Bordean, O. N., & Bunduchi, R. (2021). A systematic literature review on accelerators. *The Journal of Technology Transfer*, *46*(1), 62-89.

Davies, I. A., Haugh, H., & Chambers, L. (2019). Barriers to Social Enterprise Growth. *Journal of Small Business Management*, *57*(4), 1616-1636.

De Waele, L., Berghman, L., & Matthyssens, P. (2015). Defining Hybridity and Hybrid Contingencies in Public Organizations: An Alternative Conceptual Model. In *Contingency, Behavioural and Evolutionary Perspectives on Public and Nonprofit Governance* (Vol. 4, pp. 113-154). Emerald Group Publishing Limited.

Doherty, B., Haugh, H., & Lyon, F. (2014). Social Enterprises as Hybrid Organizations: A Review and Research Agenda. *International Journal of Management Reviews*, *16*(4), 417-436.

Domanski, D., Howaldt, J., & Kaletka, C. (2019). A comprehensive concept of social innovation and its implications for the local context – on the growing importance of social innovation ecosystems and infrastructures. *European Planning Studies*, *28*, 1-21.

Fauchart, E., & Gruber, M. (2011). Darwinians, Communitarians, and Missionaries: The Role of Founder Identity in Entrepreneurship. *Academy of Management Journal*, *54*(5), 935-957.

Fiorentino, S. (2019). Different typologies of 'co-working spaces' and the contemporary dynamics of local economic development in Rome. *European Planning Studies*, *27*(9), 1768-1790.

Fischer, R. L., Wilsker, A., & Young, D. R. (2011). Exploring the Revenue Mix of Nonprofit Organizations: Does It Relate to Publicness? *Nonprofit and Voluntary Sector Quarterly*, *40*(4), 662-681.

Foreman, P., & Whetten, D. A. (2002). Members' Identification with Multiple-Identity Organizations. *Organization Science*, *13*(6), 618-635.

Fu, J. S. (2023). Social-Market Hybridity in Social Ventures: Scale Development and Validation. *Business & Society*, *0*(0), 00076503231167569.

GALI. (2023). *The Accelerator Landscape*. GALI. Retrieved August 20 from https://www.galidata.org/accelerators/directory/

Gao, Y., & Hu, Y. (2017). The upgrade to hybrid incubators in China: a case study of Tuspark incubator. *Journal of Science and Technology Policy Management*, *8*(3), 331-351.

Gehringer, T. (2021). Corporate Foundations as Hybrid Organizations: A Systematic Review of Literature. *VOLUNTAS: International Journal of Voluntary and Nonprofit Organizations*, *32*(2), 257-275.

Glynn, M. A. (2000). When Cymbals become Symbols: Conflict over Organizational Identity within a Symphony Orchestra. *Organization Science*, *11*(3), 285-298.

Grimes, M. G., Williams, T. A., & Zhao, E. Y. (2019). Anchors Aweigh: The Sources, Variety, and Challenges of Mission Drift. *Academy of Management Review*, *44*(4), 819-845.

Hackett, S. M., & Dilts, D. M. (2004). A Systematic Review of Business Incubation Research. *The Journal of Technology Transfer*, *29*(1), 55-82.

Hagedoorn, J., Haugh, H., Robson, P., & Sugar, K. (2022). Social innovation, goal orientation, and openness: insights from social enterprise hybrids. *Small Business Economics*.

Hair, J., Hollingsworth, C. L., Randolph, A. B., & Chong, A. Y. L. (2017). An updated and expanded assessment of PLS-SEM in information systems research. *Industrial Management & Data Systems*, *117*(3), 442-458.

Hair, J., Hult, G. T. M., Ringle, C., & Sarstedt, M. (2022). *A Primer on Partial Least Squares Structural Equation Modeling (PLS-SEM)*. Thousand Oaks, CA: SAGE.

Hair, J. F., Hult, G. T. M., Ringle, C. M., Sarstedt, M., Danks, N. P., & Ray, S. (2021). *Partial Least Squares Structural Equation Modeling (PLS-SEM) Using R: A Workbook*. Cham, Switzerland: Springer.

Hair, J. F., Ringle, C. M., & Sarstedt, M. (2011). PLS-SEM: Indeed a Silver Bullet. *Journal of Marketing Theory and Practice*, *19*(2), 139-152.

Hair, J. F., Risher, J. J., Sarstedt, M., & Ringle, C. M. (2019). When to use and how to report the results of PLS-SEM. *European Business Review*, *31*(1), 2-24.

Hausberg, J. P., & Korreck, S. (2020). Business incubators and accelerators: a co-citation analysis-based, systematic literature review. *The Journal of Technology Transfer*, *45*(1), 151-176.

Hengevoss, A. (2023). Comprehensive INGO Accountability to Strengthen Perceived Program Effectiveness: A Logical Thing? *VOLUNTAS: International Journal of Voluntary and Nonprofit Organizations*.

Henseler, J., Ringle, C. M., & Sarstedt, M. (2015). A new criterion for assessing discriminant validity in variance-based structural equation modeling. *Journal of the Academy of Marketing Science*, *43*(1), 115-135.

Hirschmann, M., Moritz, A., & Block, J. H. (2021). Motives, Supporting Activities, and Selection Criteria of Social Impact Incubators: An Experimental Conjoint Study. *Nonprofit and Voluntary Sector Quarterly*, 08997640211057402.

Ho, J.-Y., & Yoon, S. (2022). Ambiguous roles of intermediaries in social entrepreneurship: The case of social innovation system in South Korea. *Technological Forecasting and Social Change*, *175*, 121324.

Howells, J. (2006). Intermediation and the role of intermediaries in innovation. *Research Policy*, *35*(5), 715-728.

Ibrahim, N. A., & Angelidis, J. P. (1995). The corporate social responsiveness orientation of board members: Are there differences between inside and outside directors? *Journal of Business Ethics*, *14*(5), 405-410.

Ibrahim, N. A., Angelidis, J. P., & Howard, D. P. (2000). The Corporate Social Responsiveness Orientation of Hospital Directors: Does Occupational Background Make a Difference? *Health Care Management Review*, *25*(2), 85-92.

Ibrahim, N. A., Howard, D. P., & Angelidis, J. P. (2008). The Relationship between Religiousness and Corporate Social Responsibility Orientation: Are there Differences Between Business Managers and Students? *Journal of Business Ethics*, *78*(1), 165-174.

Ji, C., & Konrath, S. (2023). Penalty or Reward? The Role of Hybrid Identities in Social Enterprises' Resource Acquisition. *VOLUNTAS: International Journal of Voluntary and Nonprofit Organizations*.

Jing, Y., Torenvlied, R., van Gerven, M., & Cao, J. (2021). Nonprofit contracting and partnership in elderly care: a comparison between china and the Netherlands. *Global Public Policy and Governance, 1*(2), 136-158.

Kannampuzha, M., & Hockerts, K. (2019). Organizational social entrepreneurship: scale development and validation. *Social Enterprise Journal, 15*(3), 290-319.

Kher, R., Yang, S., & Newbert, S. L. (2022). Accelerating emergence: the causal (but contextual) effect of social impact accelerators on nascent for-profit social ventures. *Small Business Economics*.

Kirtley, J., & O'Mahony, S. (2023). What is a pivot? Explaining when and how entrepreneurial firms decide to make strategic change and pivot. *Strategic Management Journal, 44*(1), 197-230.

Kock, N., & Hadaya, P. (2018). Minimum sample size estimation in PLS-SEM: The inverse square root and gamma-exponential methods. *Information Systems Journal, 28*(1), 227-261.

Kurland, N. B., & Schneper, W. D. (2021). A Social Enterprise's Hybridising Journey to Reconcile Goals and Structure with Identity. *Journal of Social Entrepreneurship*, 1-26.

Lall, S. A., Chen, L.-W., & Roberts, P. W. (2020). Are we accelerating equity investment into impact-oriented ventures? *World Development, 131*, 104952.

Lamy, E. (2019). How to Make Social Entrepreneurship Sustainable? A Diagnosis and a Few Elements of a Response. *Journal of Business Ethics, 155*(3), 645-662.

Liu, Q., & Kim, M. (2021). Benefit-Based Revenue Streams and Financial Health: The Case of Arts and Cultural Nonprofits. *Nonprofit and Voluntary Sector Quarterly, 51*(4), 805-831.

Liu, Z., & Van de Walle, S. (2023). A comparative analysis of resource networks of intermediary support organizations for nonprofit development: Evidence from incubators for nonprofit organizations. *Nonprofit Management and Leadership, 34*(2), 371-391.

Mahmoud-Jouini, S. B., Duvert, C., & Esquirol, M. (2018). Key Factors in Building a Corporate Accelerator Capability. *Research-Technology Management, 61*(4), 26-34.

Mayer, W. J., Wang, H.-c., Egginton, J. F., & Flint, H. S. (2014). The Impact of Revenue Diversification on Expected Revenue and Volatility for Nonprofit Organizations. *Nonprofit and Voluntary Sector Quarterly, 43*(2), 374-392.

Mian, S., Lamine, W., & Fayolle, A. (2016). Technology Business Incubation: An overview of the state of knowledge. *Technovation, 50-51*, 1-12.

Mongelli, L., Rullani, F., Ramus, T., & Rimac, T. (2019). The Bright Side of Hybridity: Exploring How Social Enterprises Manage and Leverage Their Hybrid Nature. *Journal of Business Ethics, 159*(2), 301-305.

Moss, T. W., Short, J. C., Payne, G. T., & Lumpkin, G. T. (2011). Dual Identities in Social Ventures: An Exploratory Study. *Entrepreneurship Theory and Practice, 35*(4), 805-830.

Nicolopoulou, K., Karataş-Özkan, M., Vas, C., & Nouman, M. (2017). An incubation perspective on social innovation: the London Hub – a social incubator. *R&D Management, 47*(3), 368-384.

Nunes, F. G., do Nascimento, G., & Martins, L. D. (2023). Do sectors (still) matter? Exploring similarities and differences between public, private, and non-profit organizations from an organizational identity perspective [online first]. *Nonprofit Management and Leadership, n/a*(n/a).

Ocasio, W. (1997). Towards an Attention-Based View of the Firm. *Strategic Management Journal*, *18*, 187-206.

Pandey, S., Lall, S., Pandey, S. K., & Ahlawat, S. (2017). The Appeal of Social Accelerators: What do Social Entrepreneurs Value? *Journal of Social Entrepreneurship*, *8*(1), 88-109.

Peng, D. X., & Lai, F. (2012). Using partial least squares in operations management research: A practical guideline and summary of past research. *Journal of Operations Management*, *30*(6), 467-480.

Powell, W. W., & Sandholtz, K. W. (2012). Amphibious entrepreneurs and the emergence of organizational forms. *Strategic Entrepreneurship Journal*, *6*(2), 94-115.

Ramus, T., Vaccaro, A., & Brusoni, S. (2016). Institutional Complexity in Turbulent Times: Formalization, Collaboration, and the Emergence of Blended Logics. *Academy of Management Journal*, *60*(4), 1253-1284.

Reinartz, W., Haenlein, M., & Henseler, J. (2009). An empirical comparison of the efficacy of covariance-based and variance-based SEM. *International Journal of Research in Marketing*, *26*(4), 332-344.

Roberts, P. W., & Lall, S. A. (2018). *Observing acceleration: Uncovering the effects of accelerators on impact-oriented entrepreneurs*. Springer.

Roundy, P. T. (2017). Hybrid organizations and the logics of entrepreneurial ecosystems. *International Entrepreneurship and Management Journal*, *13*(4), 1221-1237.

Salavou, H., & Manolopoulos, D. (2021). Pure and hybrid strategies in social enterprises: an empirical investigation. *Euromed Journal of Business*, *16*(3), 274-289.

Sansone, G., Andreotti, P., Colombelli, A., & Landoni, P. (2020). Are social incubators different from other incubators? Evidence from Italy. *Technological Forecasting and Social Change*, *158*, 120132.

Sarma, S. K. (2020). Retaining the social goal: role of path creation in for-profit social enterprises. *Journal of Management History*, *26*(1), 77-98.

Sarstedt, M., Hair, J. F., Ringle, C. M., Thiele, K. O., & Gudergan, S. P. (2016). Estimation issues with PLS and CBSEM: Where the bias lies! *Journal of Business Research*, *69*(10), 3998-4010.

Sarstedt, M., Ringle, C. M., Cheah, J.-H., Ting, H., Moisescu, O. I., & Radomir, L. (2020). Structural model robustness checks in PLS-SEM. *Tourism Economics*, *26*(4), 531-554.

Scarlata, M., & Alemany, L. (2010). Deal Structuring in Philanthropic Venture Capital Investments: Financing Instrument, Valuation and Covenants. *Journal of Business Ethics*, *95*(2), 121-145.

Schröer, A., & Jäger, U. (2015). Beyond Balancing?: A Research Agenda on Leadership in Hybrid Organizations. *International Studies of Management & Organization*, *45*(3), 259-281.

Seibel, W. (2015). Studying Hybrids: Sectors and Mechanisms. *Organization Studies*, *36*(6), 697-712.

Sentana, E., Gonzalez, R., Gasco, J., & Llopis, J. (2018). New strategies to measure and strengthen the social role of business incubators: their application to a Spanish region. *European Journal of International Management*, *12*(5-6), 536-553.

Shepherd, D. A., Williams, T. A., & Zhao, E. Y. (2019). A Framework for Exploring the Degree of Hybridity in Entrepreneurship. *Academy of Management Perspectives*, *33*(4), 491-512.

Siwale, J., Kimmitt, J., & Amankwah-Amoah, J. (2021). The Failure of Hybrid Organizations: A Legitimation Perspective. *Management and Organization Review*, *17*(3), 452-485.

Sonnino, R., & Griggs-Trevarthen, C. (2013). A resilient social economy? Insights from the community food sector in the UK. *Entrepreneurship & Regional Development*, *25*(3-4), 272-292.

Sours, P., Machado, M., & Burleson, G. (2020). Social Innovation in the USA: A Landscape Analysis of Social Enterprise Incubators. Retrieved 10 October 2022, from https://www.engineeringforchange.org/wp-content/uploads/2020/12/E4C-Villgro-Landscape-Analysis-USA.pdf

Staessens, M., Kerstens, P. J., Bruneel, J., & Cherchye, L. (2019). Data Envelopment Analysis and Social Enterprises: Analysing Performance, Strategic Orientation and Mission Drift. *Journal of Business Ethics*, *159*(2), 325-341.

Stevens, R., Moray, N., & Bruneel, J. (2015). The Social and Economic Mission of Social Enterprises: Dimensions, Measurement, Validation, and Relation. *Entrepreneurship Theory and Practice*, *39*(5), 1051-1082.

Streukens, S., & Leroi-Werelds, S. (2016). Bootstrapping and PLS-SEM: A step-by-step guide to get more out of your bootstrap results. *European Management Journal*, *34*(6), 618-632.

Stühlinger, S., & Hersberger-Langloh, S. E. (2021). Multitasking NPOs: An Analysis of the Relationship Between Funding Intentions and Nonprofit Capacities. *VOLUNTAS: International Journal of Voluntary and Nonprofit Organizations*, *32*(5), 1042-1053.

Valero, J. N., Saitgalina, M., & Black, R. A. (2021). Understanding the Nature of Non-Profit Incubators with Other Sector Incubators in the Founding of Social Change Organisations by Social Entrepreneurs. *Journal of Social Entrepreneurship*, 1-20.

Vanderstraeten, J., & Matthyssens, P. (2012). Service-based differentiation strategies for business incubators: Exploring external and internal alignment. *Technovation*, *32*(12), 656-670.

Von Schnurbein, G., & Fritz, T. M. (2017). Benefits and Drivers of Nonprofit Revenue Concentration. *Nonprofit and Voluntary Sector Quarterly*, *46*(5), 922-943.

Voss, Z. G., Cable, D. M., & Voss, G. B. (2006). Organizational Identity and Firm Performance: What Happens When Leaders Disagree about "Who We Are?". *Organization Science*, *17*(6), 741-755.

Whetten, D. A., & Mackey, A. (2002). A Social Actor Conception of Organizational Identity and Its Implications for the Study of Organizational Reputation. *Business & Society*, *41*(4), 393-414.

Wiesel, I., & Liu, F. (2021). Conceptualising modes of redistribution in public urban infrastructure. *Urban Studies*, *58*(8), 1561-1580.

Williamson, O. E. (1981). The Economics of Organization: The Transaction Cost Approach. *American Journal of Sociology*, *87*(3), 548-577.

Wilsker, A., & Young, D. (2010). How Does Program Composition Affect the Revenues of Nonprofit Organizations?: Investigating a Benefits Theory of Nonprofit Finance. *Public Finance Review*, *38*(2), 193-216.

Woodside, S. J. (2018). Dominant logics US WISEs and the tendency to favor a market-dominant or social mission-dominant approach. *Social Enterprise Journal*, *14*(1), 39-59.

Wry, T., & York, J. G. (2017). An Identity-Based Approach to Social Enterprise. *Academy of Management Review*, *42*(3), 437-460.

Yang, S., Kher, R., Newbert, S.L. (2020). What signals matter for social startups? It depends: The influence of gender role congruity on social impact accelerator selection decisions. *Journal of Business Venturing*, *35*(2).

Yin, J. L., & Chen, H. (2019). Dual-goal management in social enterprises: evidence from China. *Management Decision*, *57*(6), 1362-1381.

Young, D., Wilsker, A., & Grinsfelder, M. C. (2010). Understanding the determinants of nonprofit income portfolios. *Voluntary Sector Review*, *1*(2), 161-173.

Young, D. R. (2017). *Financing Nonprofits and Other Social Enterprises: A Benefits Approach*. Cheltenham, UK: Edward Elgar Publishing.